Genuine Men

GENUINE MEN

Journeys in Stories and Stills

Nancy Bruno

BridgewayBooks

Genuine Men: Journeys in Stories and Stills

Published by Bridgeway Books
P.O. Box 80107
Austin, Texas 78758

For more information about our books, please write to us, call 512.478.2028, or visit our website at www.bridgewaybooks.net.

Library of Congress Control Number: 2008921837

ISBN-13: 978-1-934454-27-5
ISBN-10: 1-934454-27-3

Cover photo by Nancy Bruno

Cover concept design by Priyanka Kodikal

10 9 8 7 6 5 4 3 2 1

For my sons

Table of Contents

Foreword

What is a "Man"?

Never in history has the subject of manhood been in such need of definition. For thousands of years his role was easily defined—usually in the physical terms of being the hunter, provider, breadwinner, or protector. Those who participated in wars were held up as poster boys for such definitions, and they would be introduced to young boys as heroes. Growing up as a man in the last third of the twentieth century was thrilling, confusing, challenging, and frustrating, filled with unbelievable highs and brutal lows. When I was a child, well-dressed Marines would drive their government vehicles down the street, and I saluted proudly, as any eight-year-old boy would. I watched with wishful eyes as men with "The Right Stuff" raced to the moon "not because it was easy… but because it was hard." I would reenact the "Immaculate Reception" (Pittsburgh Steelers) thousands of times on sandlots surrounded by imaginary stadiums of 80,000 fans screaming my name. It was easy to define a man back then. But then it all changed. In the latter half of the century, women redefined their roles in society, and for most of those decades the focus was on them and their struggles. The liberation would turn the world on its head. But for men? A definition? No one really worried about it. How a "real man" was defined was a humorous subject that did not get the real attention it deserved.

I am just now, at forty-eight, really coming to grips what a real man is all about. I have arrived at this destination after experiencing some of the most difficult and painful years of my life. Is it a coincidence that in the middle of my struggle I was selected to be part of this enviable list of "great men"? I think not. The project forced me, for the first time, to think about what I might look like from the outside in. It suggested that my privately held beliefs should be shared, as they have—and continue to—save my life. What could be manlier than saving lives? What could be more courageous than opening up your most private thoughts to others?

As part of a dying and rare breed, I am profoundly flattered to be included in what may be part of the defining process of what a man is. Yes, he is brave and heroic and still very physical. But he is introspective and understands the magic and the power of his thoughts. He balances his thoughts and desires with the women who surround him and share his path. He is a beacon of hope to those who struggle with their faith and beliefs. He sets an example for those he loves and even for those who don't love him. A true man never surrenders to negative thought. Welcome to my new definition.

—Jimmy Tanico

A Book for Men

When Nancy asked me to be part of this project, I wasn't sure what to expect. I knew her as a person but had never directly experienced her professional work. We certainly discussed it and shared our stories and successes, but in the way friends do, just keeping each other informed about our lives. When she gave me the honor to participate, I learned something incredible about who I am. Nancy provided me with the gift of forcing me to see myself from the inside, but through other people's eyes. Many of us never have the opportunity in our lifetime to think about how we are viewed by those around us, and through *Genuine Men,* I got to do that at thirty-eight years of age.

This book will provide a great gift to the world. Every person who reads it, buys it for a dad, brother, son, or friend will be performing a "Mitzvah," or a commandment to do good deeds as it is known in the Jewish faith. The message of this book to me is you must know who you are to the world. What type of father, husband, boss, employee, son, brother, friend, confidant, or community member do you want to be? How do the people you interact with view you? If you don't see yourself in their eyes the way you want to be perceived, this book can show you how to change, and, in the process, live the full, and meaningful life you strive for. None of the men in this book are perfect, we all have our flaws and foibles, but there was something in each of us that was worth putting down on paper to share. I thank Nancy for giving me this incredible gift, and for having the talent and commitment to bring this message to everyone who reads or learns about this book.

—Mitch Skyer

The Stories

What does it really mean to be a man? It is a process for some, a journey for others, and at times an unreachable star. Within this book are some of the amazing roads men have traveled to earn that very precise title of "Man,"

"Father," "Husband," "Son," and "Friend." We highlight joyous times in our lives and find comfort in knowing that we lived through the dark times.

"What does it really mean to be a Man?" Have a seat, and we will tell you our stories.

—Bryant Williams

Preface

When men are little boys, there is very little consciousness of society's ideals and desires for measuring a man's success or failure—the underlying basis for designating a man as a role model. Today, a man's success or failure is often measured by his job, bank account, car, and home. Are such material measurements a true reflection of what it means to be a good role model, to have strength of character? It is time to change the way that men are defined and judged by society. Readers of *Genuine Men* will see that the men within this book truly are role models for all because of the way they've met life's challenges. They are our fathers, sons, brothers, husbands, neighbors, colleagues, and friends. They are the people you see going to work every day, watching a game with friends, barbequing in the summertime, or working out at the gym. They have experienced joy and pain, war and peace, addiction and sobriety, racism and acceptance. Their images and voices represent the genuine men that live among us every day.

I am always asked the same two questions: (1) where I get the ideas for my projects and (2) where do I find my subjects? In the case of *Genuine Men*, there was no single event that led to the creation of this project. In fact, it was a series of encounters that led me to believe that this project needed to be completed and brought to the public's attention. The spark was ignited when my oldest son, a wonderful boy with a strong sense of self approached me as I completed my work on *Beautiful Women*, my first book in this series exploring a redefinition of what it means for a woman to be beautiful. He kept track of my work and was the only person I shared any of the images with until the completed project was ready to be unveiled. It was something special that only we shared—a mother and her son. One afternoon he walked into my office and, in a very serious tone, boldly stated, "Mommy, I have been thinking. It is only fair that you do the same for boys as you did for girls." I was taken aback. In my son's innocence, all I could hear was the mantra of my maternal grandmother: "You can't do for one and not the other." It was in that moment that the "boy book," as it is lovingly called in our house, was born. Months passed, and I found myself concluding an interview with a local reporter about *Beautiful Women* when she asked me if I thought the project would have taken on a different form if my subjects were men instead of women. I took a moment. Remembering the promise I made to my son to write the boy book, I said that I would keep her number and call her one day to let her know the answer to that question. Again, time passed, and I was traveling with the Beautiful Women Project when a very tall man rushed up to me and asked if I was the person who created the exhibition. "I heard that you are going to be doing men next, and I would like to be in the project," he said. I hadn't told anyone about my next project—how did he know about the boy book? Surprised by his insider knowledge and determination, I politely took his name and contact details and let him know that I would be in touch when I began the project. This third encounter let me know it was time to get to work on the boy book.

The thirty-five men of this project range in age from twelve years old to ninety-one years old. They come from a variety of backgrounds, socioeconomic classes, races, cultures, and parts of the world. I *met* them through previous contacts, chance meetings, introductions, and—like the man at the exhibition—some found me. I came to *know* them through listening to their stories and through very open and frank discussions. I had the great honor to be in the company of men, regardless of their stage in life, who had handled their experiences in ways that made them stronger human beings. Despite their individual differences, they all share one thing in common: I know that if my sons had only twenty minutes with any of these men, they would walk away with life lessons that would help them be better men throughout their lifetime.

And that is what *Genuine Men* is all about: men with great strength of character, men who society should consider role models because of the way they approach, deal with, and then carry their life experiences. Just as I wrote in my preface for *Beautiful Women*, I believe that by bringing the images and stories of these men to the community, readers of *Genuine Men* will walk away with a new understanding of the kind of men we as a society should define as positive role models—the type of men we might want to emulate sometime in our own life journey. This new, or redefined, definition of what I believe is a display of strength of character will not only come as a result of viewing the photographs and reading the biographies but by the dialogue that will again be fostered by readers and others who hear about what is being shared within these pages. Most importantly, by seeing men in all stages of their life's journey, I want men who are struggling with the process of establishing their personal identity to realize that they are not alone in their struggle. There may be a man closer than they believe who they can look to in their quest to be good men.

There is a great deal for all of us to learn from the journey of men, regardless if we are a man or a woman. The men who fill these pages are genuine men, individuals who we can all learn from. Each one deserves of the distinction "role model," although not one thinks of himself in this way, not fully conscious of the impact that he has on those around him. These men just see themselves as ordinary, living their lives moment by moment, day by day. *Genuine Men*.

To Be a Boy

If you watch him on the soccer field, Christopher looks just like all of the other boys on his team: giving it 100 percent on the field, but goofing around with his teammates when the coach's attention is elsewhere. In school he is like any other kid trying to make it through junior high: a good student in the classes he enjoys, but scrambling to get homework done on the bus. Christopher enjoys teaching younger kids how to play new games but often becomes frustrated when his younger sister won't follow the rules. He uses his imagination to build all kinds of things with Legos; he is thinking about becoming a mechanical engineer when he grows up. And then there is Rufus, his dog. It is hard work raising a puppy: training him, walking him, and keeping him out of trouble. There have been times when it would have been easy to pass these responsibilities on to someone else—like when Rufus misbehaves or needs to be walked in the rain—but you can't just

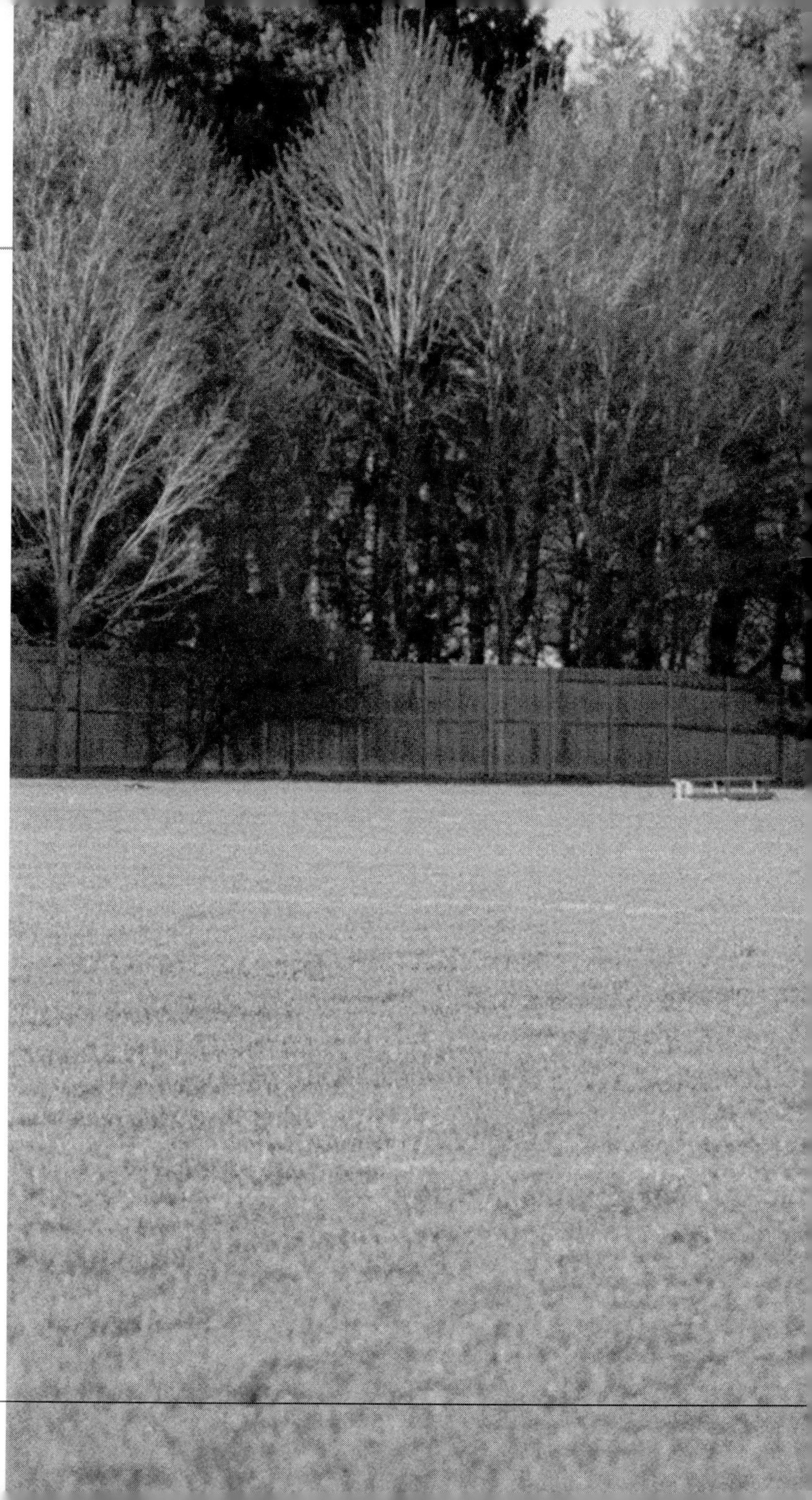

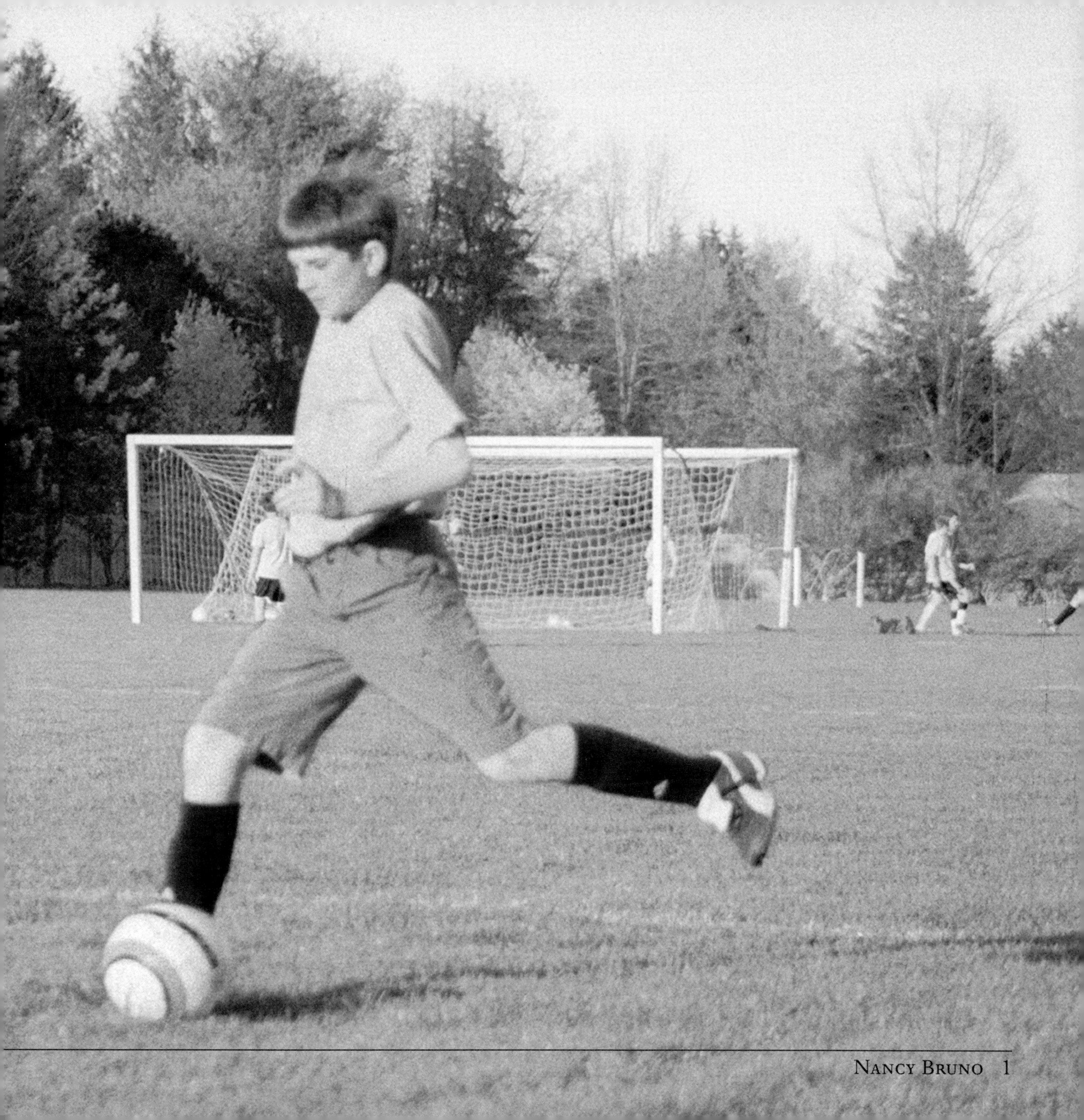

give up on someone, or in this case something, just because he isn't perfect. This is a hard lesson to learn for a boy still so young. When it comes down to it, though, Christopher loves just being a kid: pancakes with lots of syrup for breakfast, hanging out with his friends during recess, unexpected days off from school in the winter, watching the Red Sox play on the television, cannonballs into the pool and hamburgers from the grill on a warm summer's night, camping under the stars with his family. When you're just a boy, it's hard to imagine life can get any better.

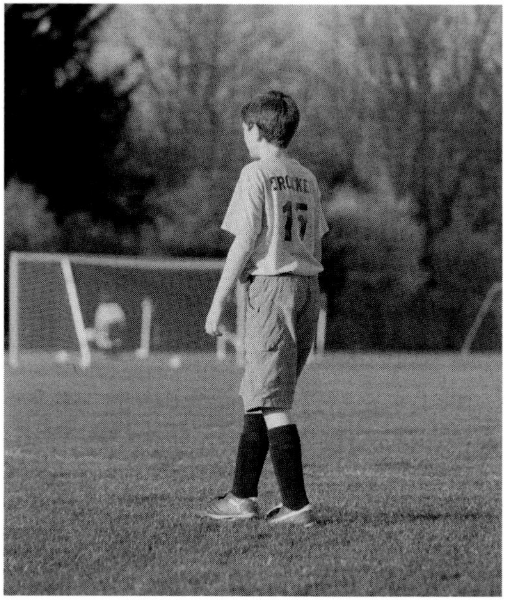

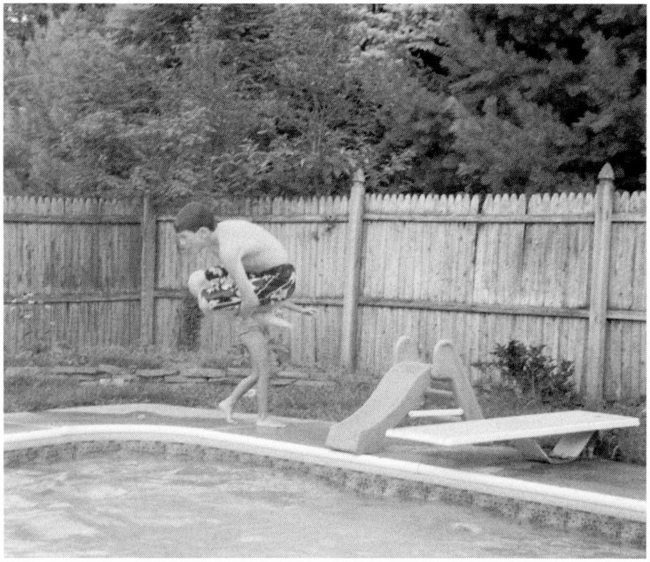

Going for It

At sixteen, Brian is balancing schoolwork and athletics, is trying to fit in and make friends at a new high school, and has the occasional disagreement with his parents. The decision to transfer high schools was a difficult one. Ultimately it came down to one thing: he wants to be the best that he can be in all aspects of his life.

When Brian was twelve years old his baseball team didn't make the World Series; they lost in the regional finals. Brian pledged from that day forward he would always give 100 percent of himself—for himself and for any team of which he was a member. When Brian was a freshman, a friend convinced him to try out for the cross country running team. When he showed up at the team's first practice, he didn't even have running shoes or shorts. He viewed it as a way to get in shape for basketball, but he was hardly a runner. At the end of the season Brian went back to playing basketball and baseball, not giving running any more thought.

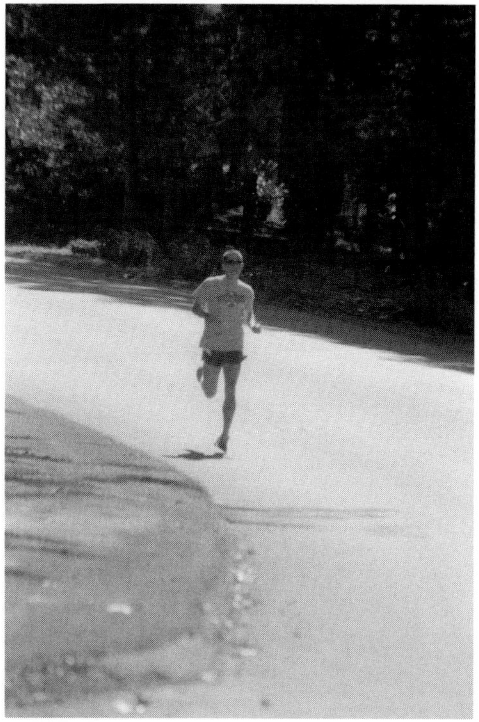

The following summer arrived, and his mom introduced him to her running group. These athletes accepted Brian and treated him as an equal despite his age and inexperience. From these men and women he not only learned about the sport of running, he learned about himself. He became hooked on running. His running role model, Steve Prefontaine, didn't run to win or to put on a show but to give his best effort. His race philosophy was simple: run hard throughout the entire race and never hold back. Brian now applies this strategy to his races and to his life. As a high school junior he is taking three college-level courses and running on the varsity cross country team. Almost as soon as that wraps up he begins indoor track, studying for and taking his SATs, and then it's outdoor track

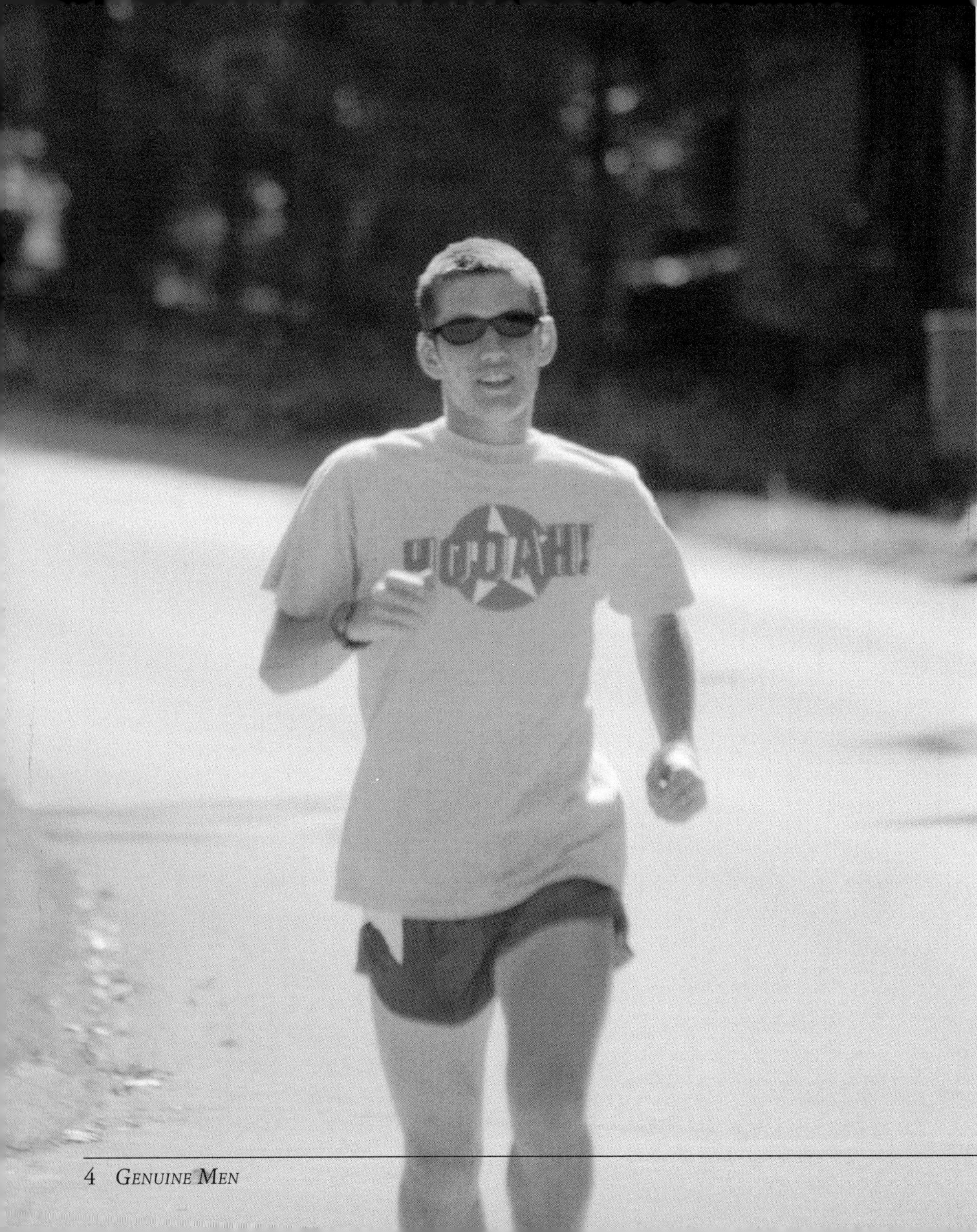
HOOAH!

season in the spring. Brian has set very definite goals for his future. Nike Team Nationals and the state and national competitions for indoor track and outdoor track, receive a scholarship offer from a Division One college and maybe even compete one day on the world stage. Brian knows exactly what he has to do to achieve those dreams. Never taking himself too seriously, he will enjoy his high school years with friends, take time to be with his family, and go out running just to have fun.

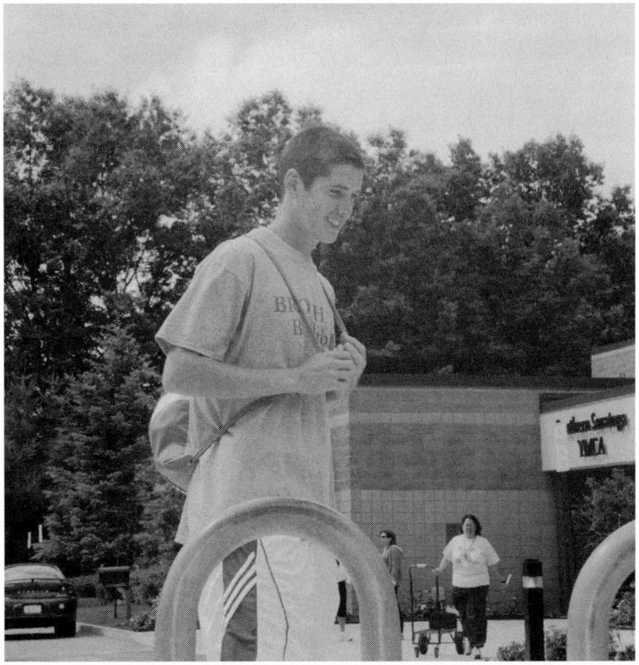

Emerging

Alex is a teenager: no longer a kid, not quite an adult. He is a work in progress, merging childhood lessons with new notions and life experiences. Always an inquisitive child, now he's like a human chemistry experiment: all of the elements of his life poured into a beaker with the hope that they will react without exploding. Ideas and thoughts are constantly zooming around in his mind, and Alex easily finds himself getting in his own way. Instead of fighting his nature, he found the debate team to be an outlet for his quick mind.

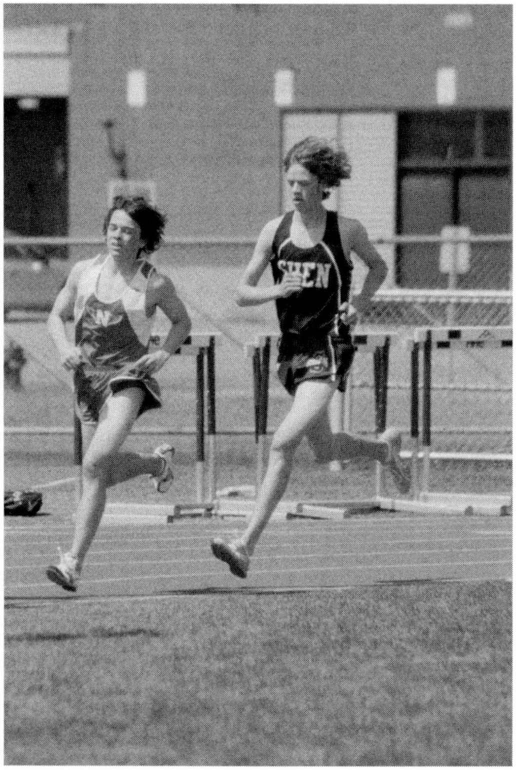

When Alex was a kid, running was about simple things like spending time with his dad going around the block, getting around the playground quickly, and winning ribbons for field day races. He only joined the cross country team in middle school because it was something to do with people he liked hanging out with after school. But now he recognizes that running is a defining part of who he is as an individual; it is about focus and drive, being invested in the outcome, and it provides him with a concrete sense of achievement.

Not all of Alex's victories are as immediate as in a race or debate. And as part of the instant-gratification generation, waiting to see the fruits of his labors can be excruciating. Alex has been working to get into a good college, and the time has finally come to see if his hard work has paid off. There is little doubt that he will go to a college; the question is will the college that he wants to attend want him? In the event that things don't turn out exactly as he wishes, he won't dwell on what he could have done in the past that may have led to a different outcome. Instead, he will go

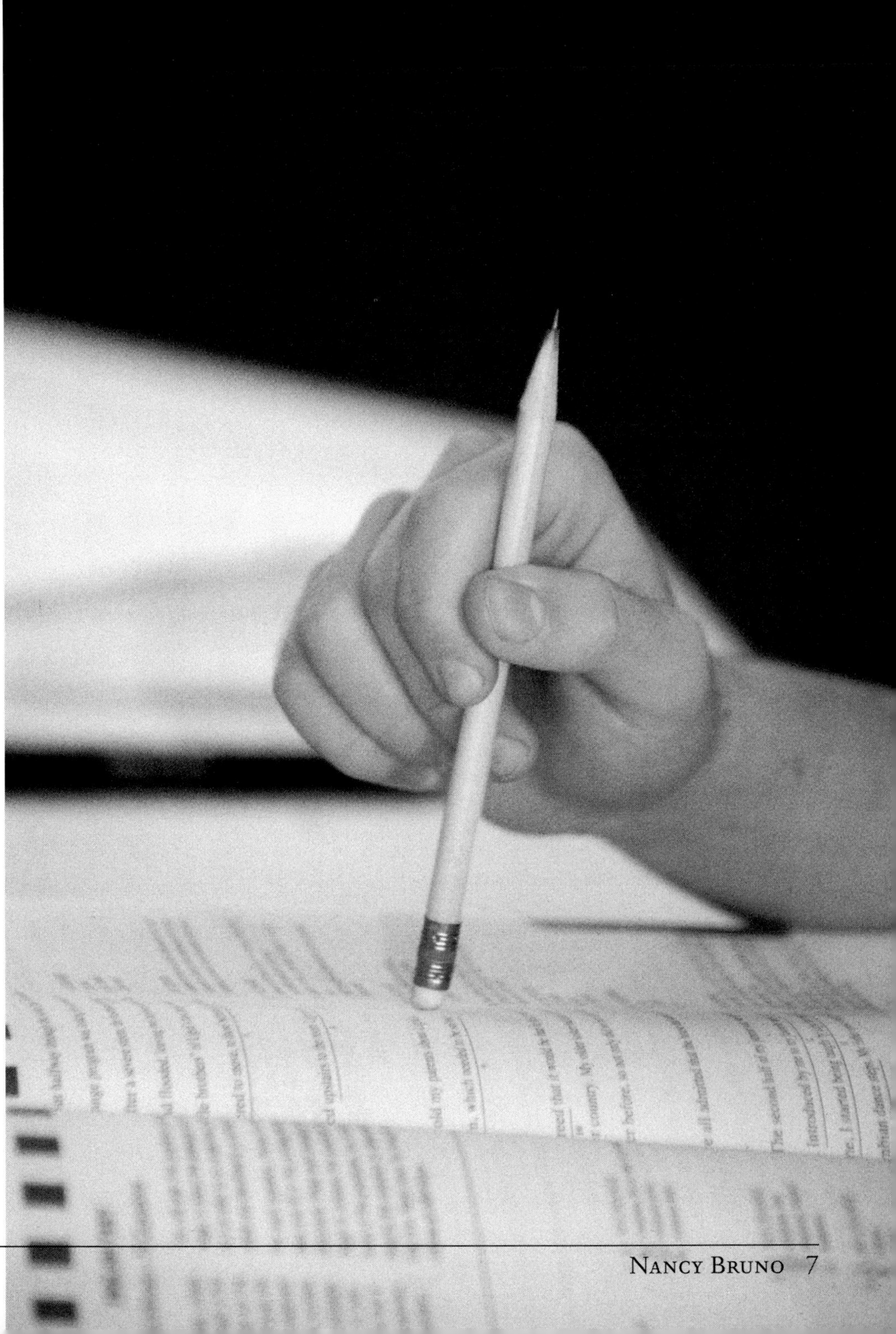

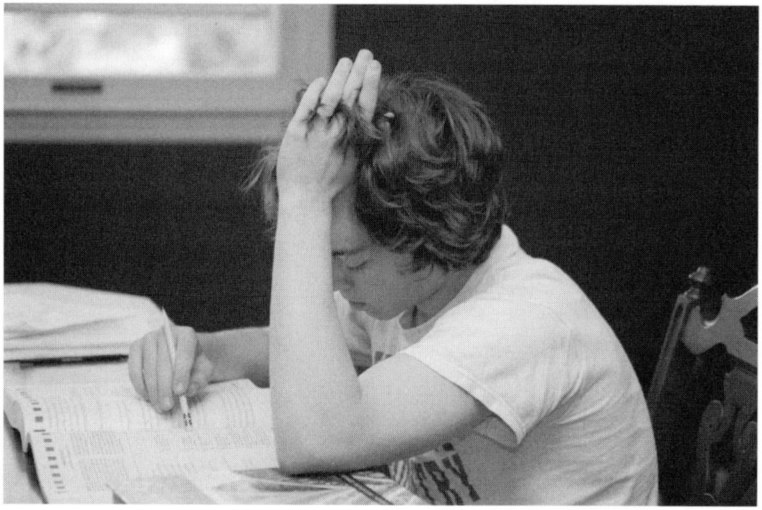

into his head and review the tapes of his high school years to understand what changes he should make within himself in order to succeed in future endeavors. The cycle will repeat itself over and over again throughout his life, merging his past lessons with new experiences. Ultimately he will emerge as the man he was meant to be.

Life Imitates Art

Maybe it was the look of the guitar, maybe it was the sound coming from the guitar—to this day he still isn't sure, and it doesn't matter. Either way, it was a transformational experience. He got his first guitar at fourteen and began by learning chords—stretching his fingers across the nape of his guitar, working them into calloused appendages. Like an athlete, he spent hours learning dexterity, building speed, and practicing agility. As he trained his ear to hear tone, melody, and rhythm, he began stringing chords together to play songs. There was no urgency to learn how to read music; the concert was always playing in his head. Dave taught himself every Pearl Jam song he knew, and through his early teens expressed himself through the songs that defined and reflected his life in so many ways: structured formulas with few progressions. As Dave began to mature, as an adolescent and a musician, he was attracted to classic rock songs. It was a natural progression; the sound provided opportunities for stylistic freedom within a construction—limited spaces to take calculated musical risks without altering the melodic nature of the song. College was just like the music: an institution that provided a place where he had the freedom of structured risk taking. In his mind, those four defined years were about self-discovery. Could those experiences really alter the landscape of the rest of his life? He was introduced to philosophies of the world and studied Buddhism, but the most important lesson he learned was that every action alters the course of a lifetime. Before he knew it four years had flown by, but instead of graduating college with his friends or traveling the country with his band, Dave was working to provide for his newborn son.

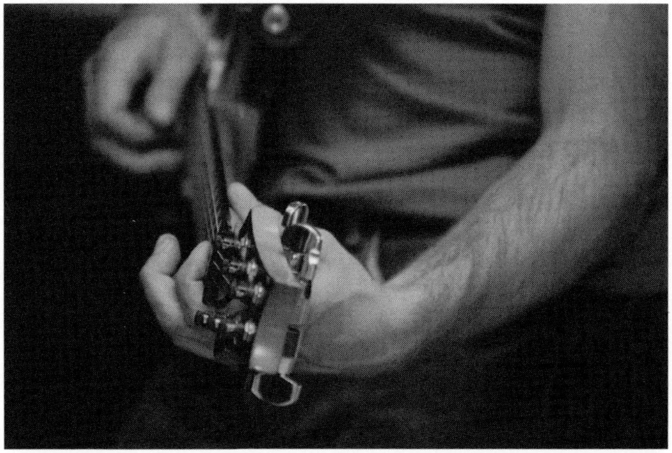

Today, he has no choice but to live in a series of improvised moments: he is a single dad juggling

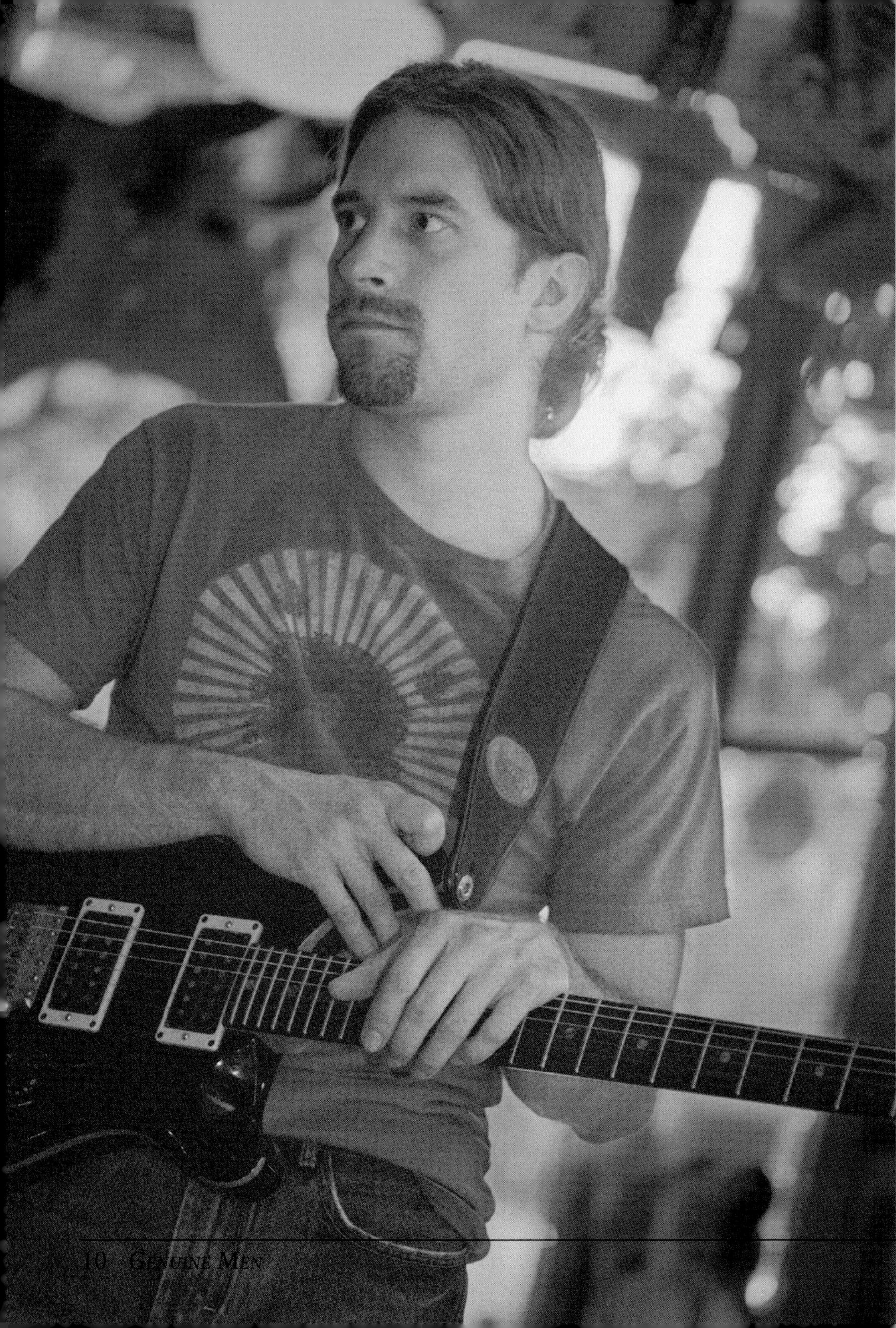

work, school, and the life questions of a five-year-old boy. Music, as it has throughout his life, grounds and defines him in the best of ways. He now plays in a funk-jazz band: a fusion of sounds and rhythms that only works when all of the musicians are in synch. Art imitates life, and for Dave music and life are one in the same: incredible, mysterious experiences that have taken him places that he would never have imagined or expected, but would have no other way.

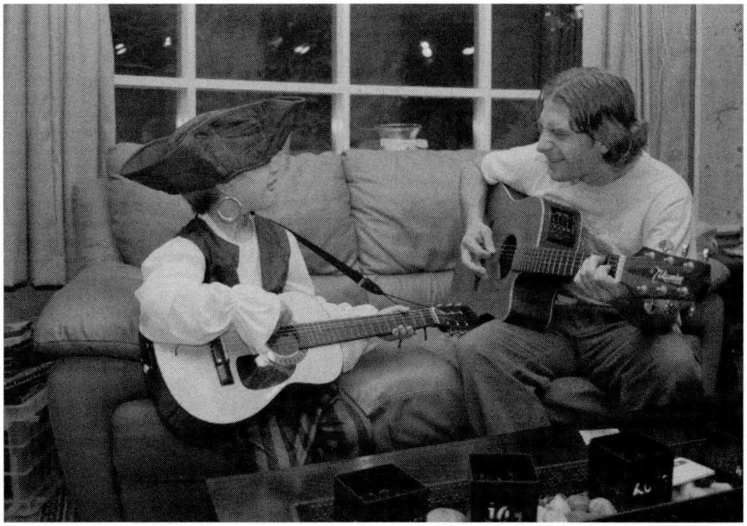

Awakening Within

His brother was known as the smart one, and his sister was the baby of the family. As a young boy, Dave became frustrated by the constant comparisons to his siblings. Despite his parents' reassuring words that they loved him for who *he* was, it is sometimes easier to believe things coming from an objective outsider. It took some time for Dave to learn that what others say or think doesn't matter; what does matter is what is within. His childhood ambitions were to be a G.I. Joe, a professional baseball player, or an architect. Somewhere along the way the first two fell by the wayside, and at college Dave began studying to be an architect. The professor of his first semester of basic design and math class told him, within the first few classes, that Dave would never find success as an architect. Intellectually, Dave knew that he should not take any stock in what a virtual stranger had to say, but coming from a person in a position of authority, the pronouncement made him question his direction. For the next two years Dave continued to lose his focus. He lost touch with himself.

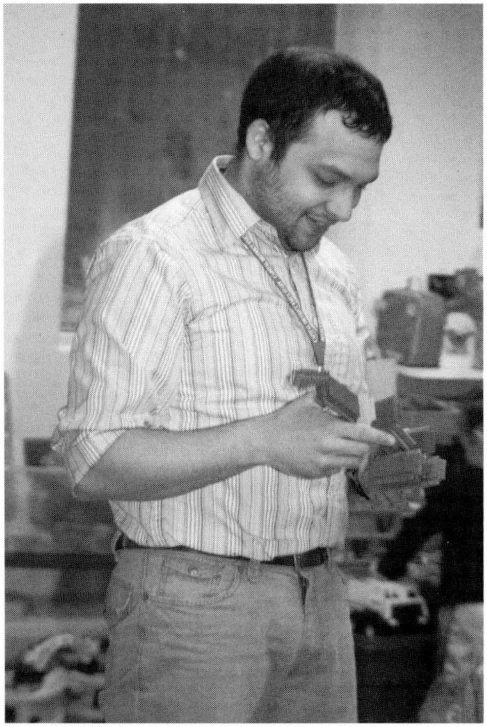

After returning home for the summer after a very tumultuous sophomore year, his best friend's father sat Dave and his own son down for a very serious discussion. To this day, his tone resonates in Dave's mind: "You are both throwing your lives away…because you fear failure." Six days later his best friend's father died of a heart attack. Devastated, Dave needed to make amends for disappointing a man who believed in him more than he believed in himself.

As Dave continued finding his way, he was drawn to a class about Thomas Merton, a Trappist monk. At the core of Merton's writings is the search for "true self": everything one needs is within one's self.

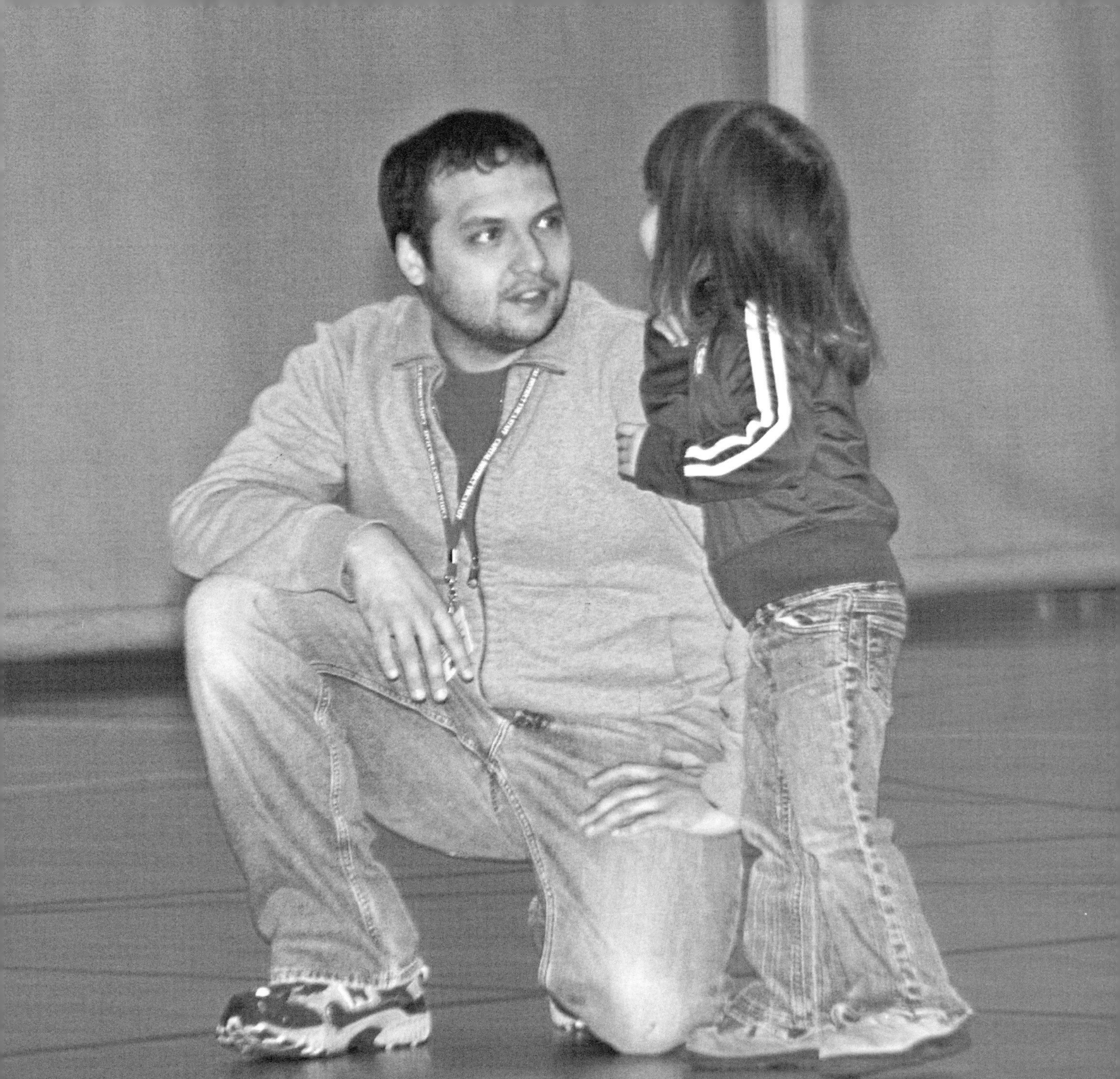

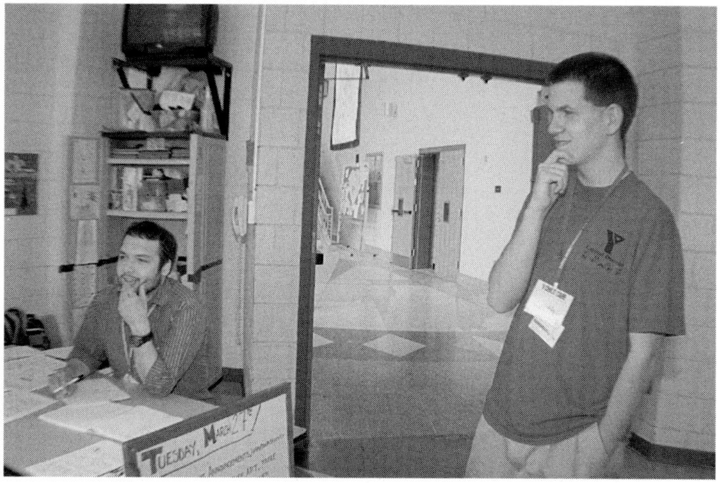

It was a message Dave had heard from various people throughout his life: his parents and grandparents, his siblings and friends, teachers and coaches, his best friend's father. Maybe it was just the right moment. Maybe it was because it came from a man who was also looked upon as a bit of a lost soul in his early years. The reason doesn't really matter. This time he knew that this was the key to his own awakening.

In just a few years, his life has taken form. His fiancée is someone who understands and loves him for who he was as a child and teenager, the person he is today, and the man who he will become as they spend their life together. A person who sees Dave walking down the street would never guess that he willingly and happily works with children every day. Most people just don't expect a man to do this job. The preschoolers he works with are inspiring, energizing, and uplifting. He teaches the older kids in his after-school program that if they believe in themselves they can accomplish anything. Taking a page from his own book, he reassures all of them that everyone eventually finds their way.

Generation Y Can't I?

Perched atop a giant boulder, seated on his mountain bike, Erik looks over the crevice and wonders, "Why can't I?" A defining phrase. The essence of who he is as an individual. As a kid Erik was always taught that he could accomplish anything he put his mind to. Watching his father renovate their home and camp, Erik often asked, "Why can't I help?" Instead of standing by and watching him do all of the work, Erik picked up the hammer and worked side by side with his father. Knowing the importance his family placed on education, throughout high school he wondered, "Why can't I attend the college of my choice?" Instead of just wondering, he chose to work hard, earning a scholarship to a private university. As a geology major his freshman year, Erik wondered what it would be like to study a volcano firsthand. "Why can't I go to Hawaii?" he asked his parents. Despite knowing their stance, Erik decided to follow his heart and applied to a college in Hawaii, sold his car, and took out a school loan. Soon after making this decision, he stepped off an airplane, five thousand miles from home, and began his sophomore year. Now he was eager to explore life's possibilities, and when a friend asked Erik if he would like to go to Alaska for a summer job he responded with the familiar "Why can't I?"

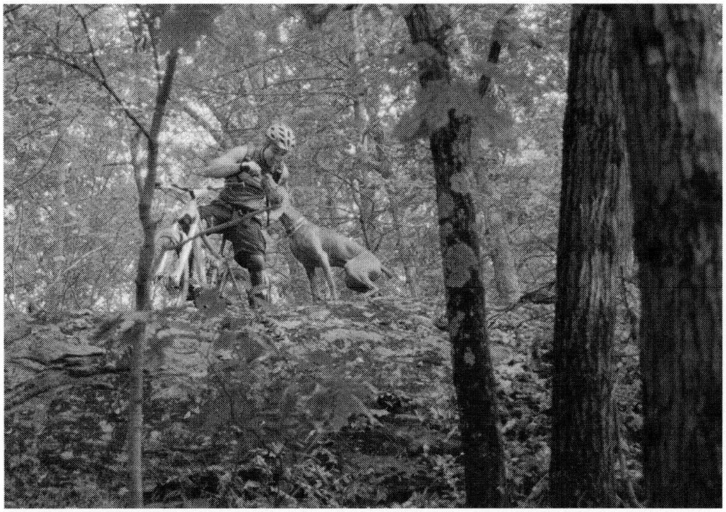

Inspired by his travels, the question arose, "Why can't I study abroad?" Pushing his boundaries as far as his imagination let him, he chose a program based in the country of Kenya. The reality of it all was completely unimaginable. All Erik could come up with was, "Why can't I make life better for these people?" His response was a plan outlining a not-for-profit organization focusing its efforts on HIV/AIDS education and water and trade

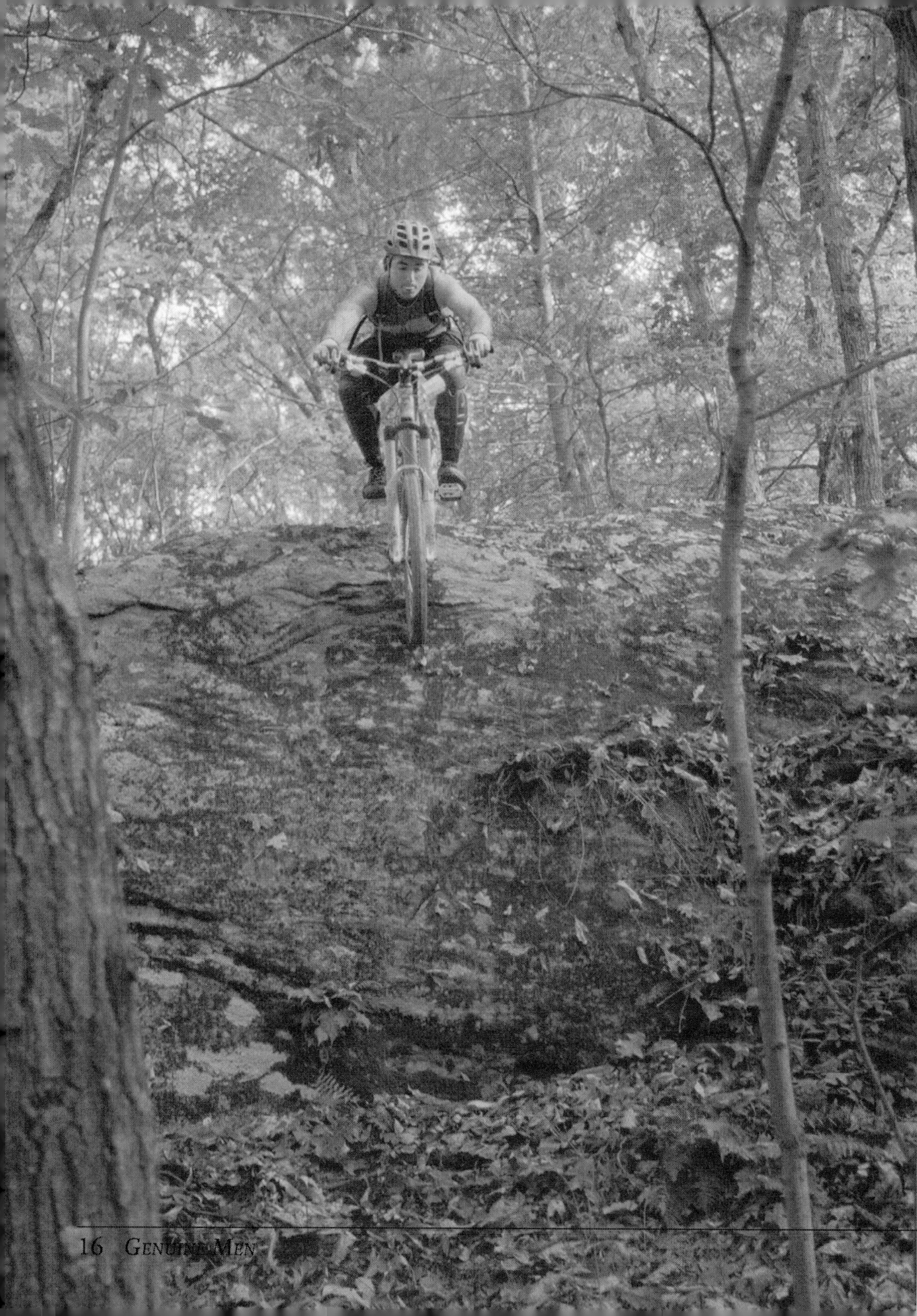

education programs. Erik's ability to identify avenues of possibility allowed him to create this profound opportunity and to share the true beauty of his "Why can't I?" mentality. Life has been like a dream come true for Erik. He has had the privilege to pursue diverse experiences in his young lifetime, and he is not done. Knowing that he has the power and capabilities to make anything happen, when faced with challenges he only has to ask himself, "Why can't I?"

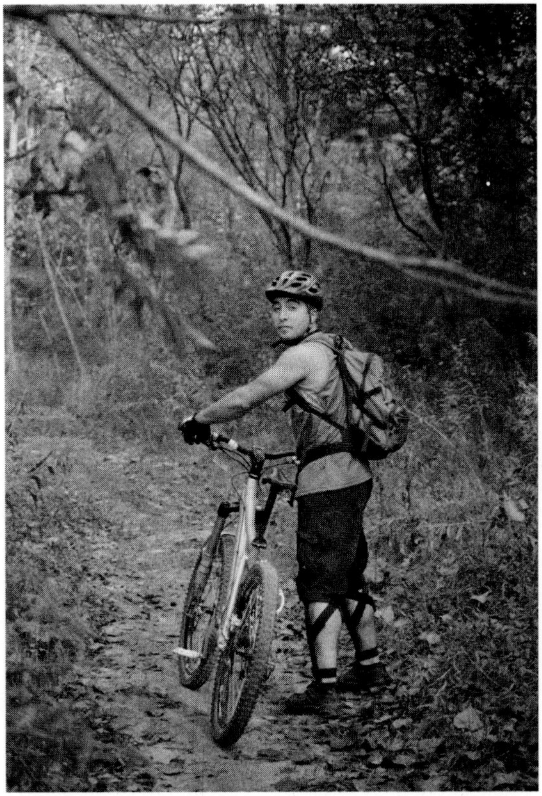

Finding His Own Way

They are simple reminders of who he is and where he comes from: his reflection in the bathroom mirror, the tattoos on his arms, a bowl of phở. Leighton is one of seven children of hard-working Vietnamese refugees. Forced from their homeland at the end of the Vietnam War, they came to the United States in search of a life for themselves, their children, and their children's children. His father attended school while working full time to support the family while his mother raised the family in their newly adopted culture and country. They settled in Southern California, an area that was home to 25,000 gangs with a total population of 200,000 members.

Growing up, gang life was part of the landscape. There were so many neighborhood kids in gangs, it just seemed normal for Leighton to hang out with them. The gang represented family and community, and there was a tremendous amount of pride in knowing that people depended upon him. Leighton's best friend was killed at the age of fourteen, a victim of a gang murder. Leighton was still just a kid himself, and the shock left him angry and numb. Until then the gang was about brotherhood, not violence. In time he realized that nothing was going to bring his friend back.The gang gave his life purpose. He saw no reason to leave. Instead, he chose to drop out of high school.

Those four years when he should have been studying math or history, playing on a sports team, going to school dances, or attending graduation, he was in and out of juvenile detention centers. Viewing

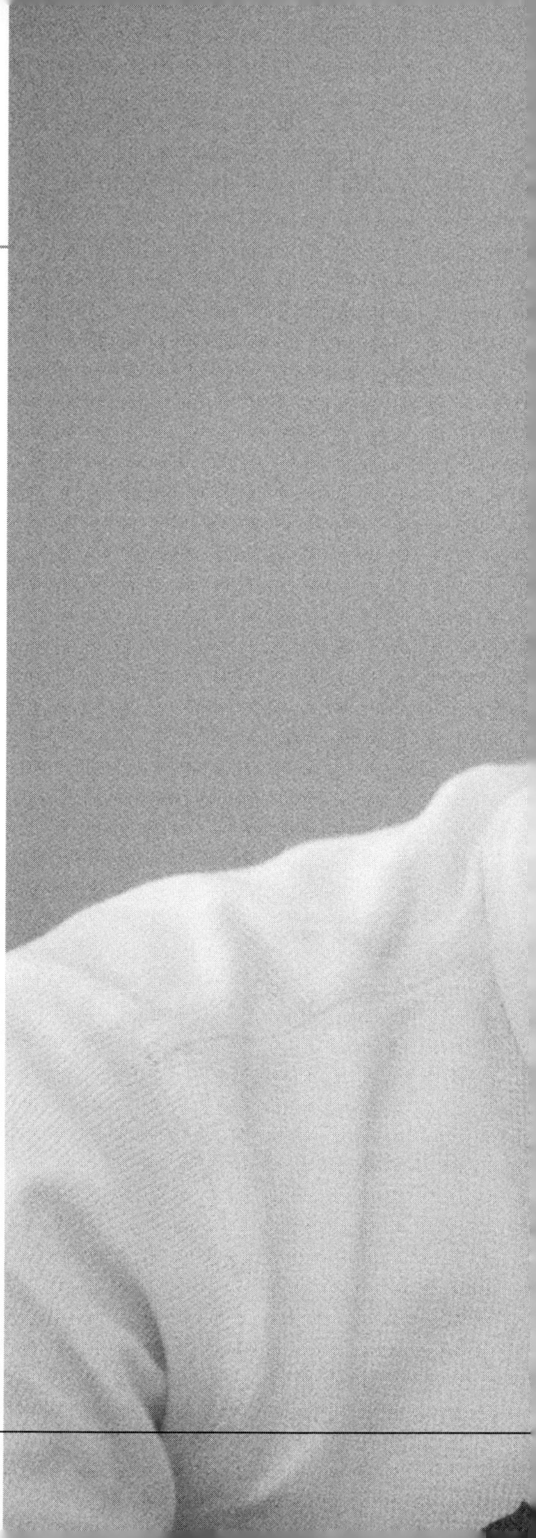

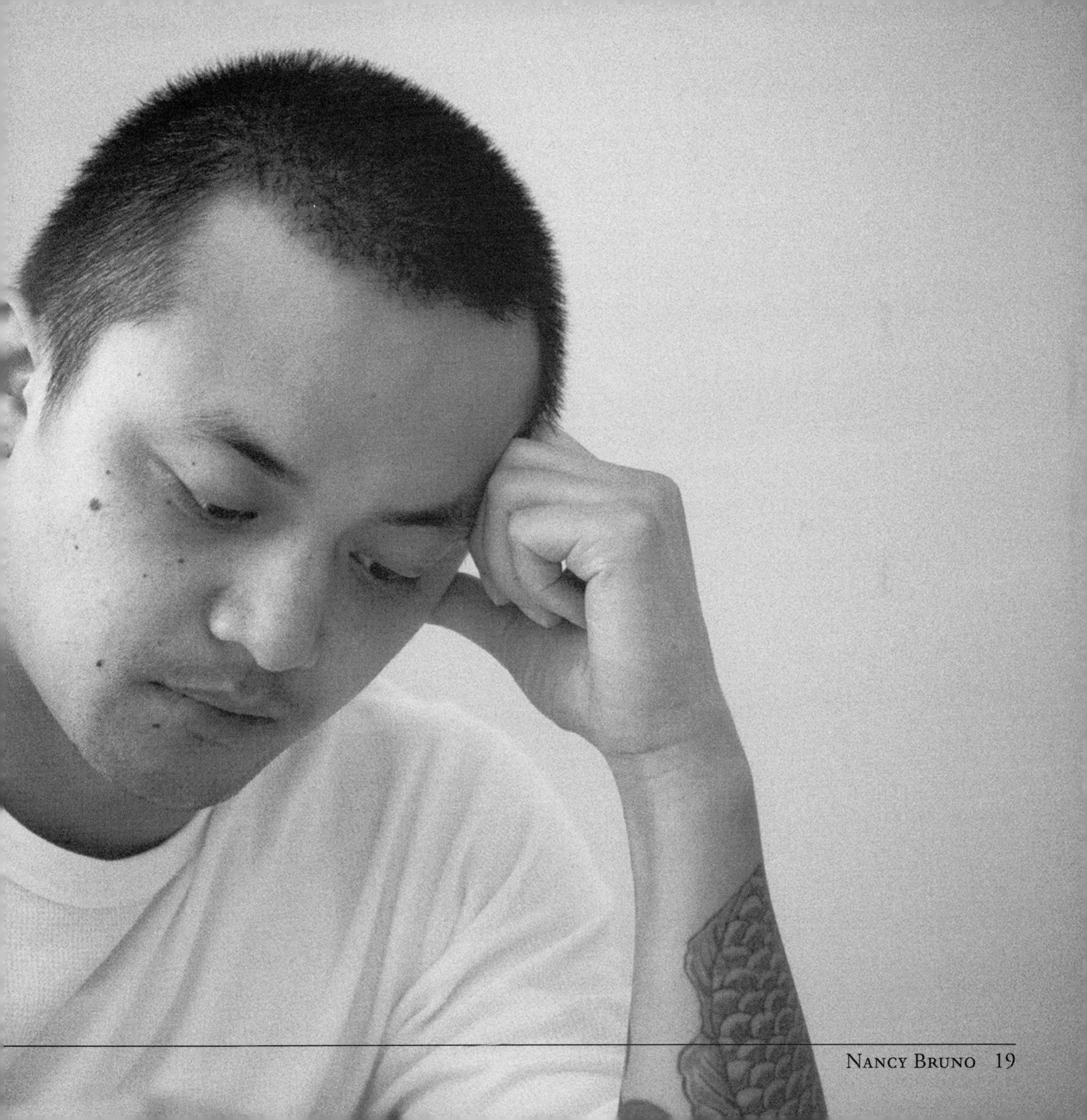

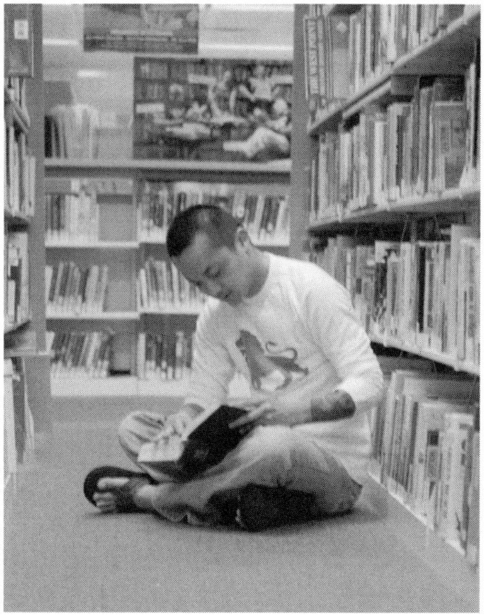

this period of his life as what shaped who he is today, Leighton refuses to be ashamed of the time he spent in juvenile detention and jail. It has turned out to be one of his most important learning experiences. While living inside a juvenile facility, he was not exposed to anything that could further corrupt him: no money, no material goods, no excuses. It was during a year's stretch in and out of juvenile detention that his daughter was born. At the age of eighteen, he had something other than himself to live for. It was time to utilize his vision to see what was in front of him, around him, and within.

He decided to leave the gang lifestyle, taking with him only the best of memories. He would never deny those years, but he was determined to make that his history, not his present or future. Knowing that it was up to him now to make a good life for his children, he taught himself the skills he needed to make his life. With no one to teach him or to root for him, he spent nights alone pouring over books about engine mechanics, design and drawing, sound production, and computer programming. There was a great deal of satisfaction in seeing the results of his own hard work and the realization of something that he created with his mind and hands.

Given the opportunity, Leighton wouldn't change anything about his life. If he did, how could he be 100 percent proud of all of his accomplishments? He is a living example that hardships are there to teach, not to lecture. They must be viewed as lessons, and only through trial and error, good times and bad, will you find how to fit those lessons into your life. His outlook may appear too unreal, too positive. For that he has all of the negatives in his life to thank and appreciate.

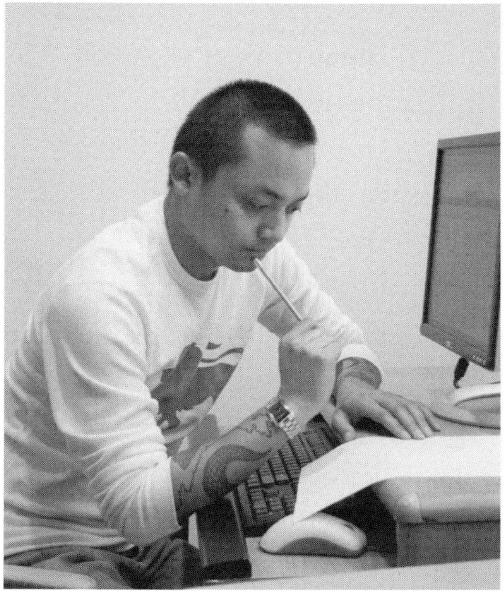

His Work Is Never Done

When you pass Humberto on the street, it is hard to imagine that at just thirty years old he leads a global ministry. As part of a faith-based outreach, Humberto ministers to anyone who shows up at his doorstep, regardless if they are Christian, Catholic, Evangelic, Muslim…everyone needs guidance and support in their time of need. The pulpit from which he preaches is not enclosed by physical walls but is surrounded by barns filled with thoroughbred race horses. The floor is not made of shiny marble but dirt and mud. There is no organ filling the sanctuary but music from all over the world coming from radios playing throughout the backstretch.

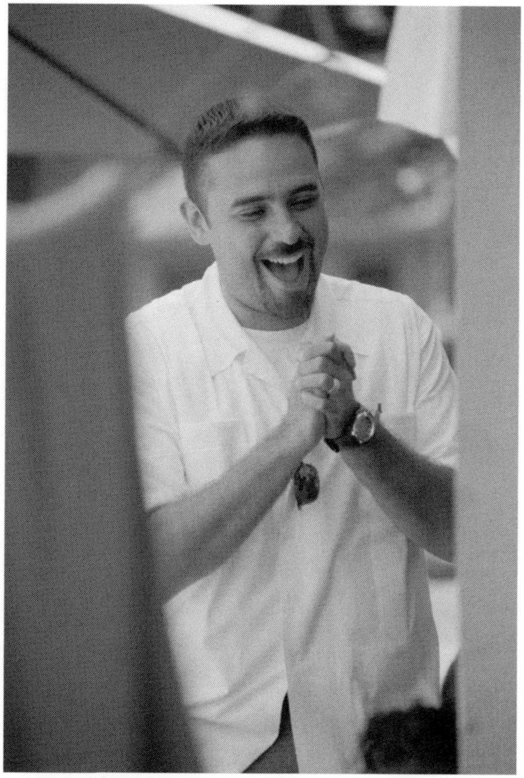

The first time he worked in the backstretch he was twelve years old, planting flowers for a horse owner. He would do his job and leave at the end of the day. He was offered the position as the racetrack chaplain when he was twenty-six. As an outsider, Humberto was suspected of being many things: part of immigration service, a policeman, a detective, and even a lawyer. It didn't occur to anyone that he was the new chaplain.

Despite that Humberto was a Mexican American and communicated in Spanish and English, his tightly knit community did not automatically welcome him into the fold. He was going to have to earn their trust, and he did it the only way he knew how: by treating and loving them as he treated and loved himself. In time, they came to depend on him for everything: marriage counseling, visas and work permits, getting a post office box, home and hospital visits, social services, getting a car fixed so they can get to work, making sure that children have clothes and

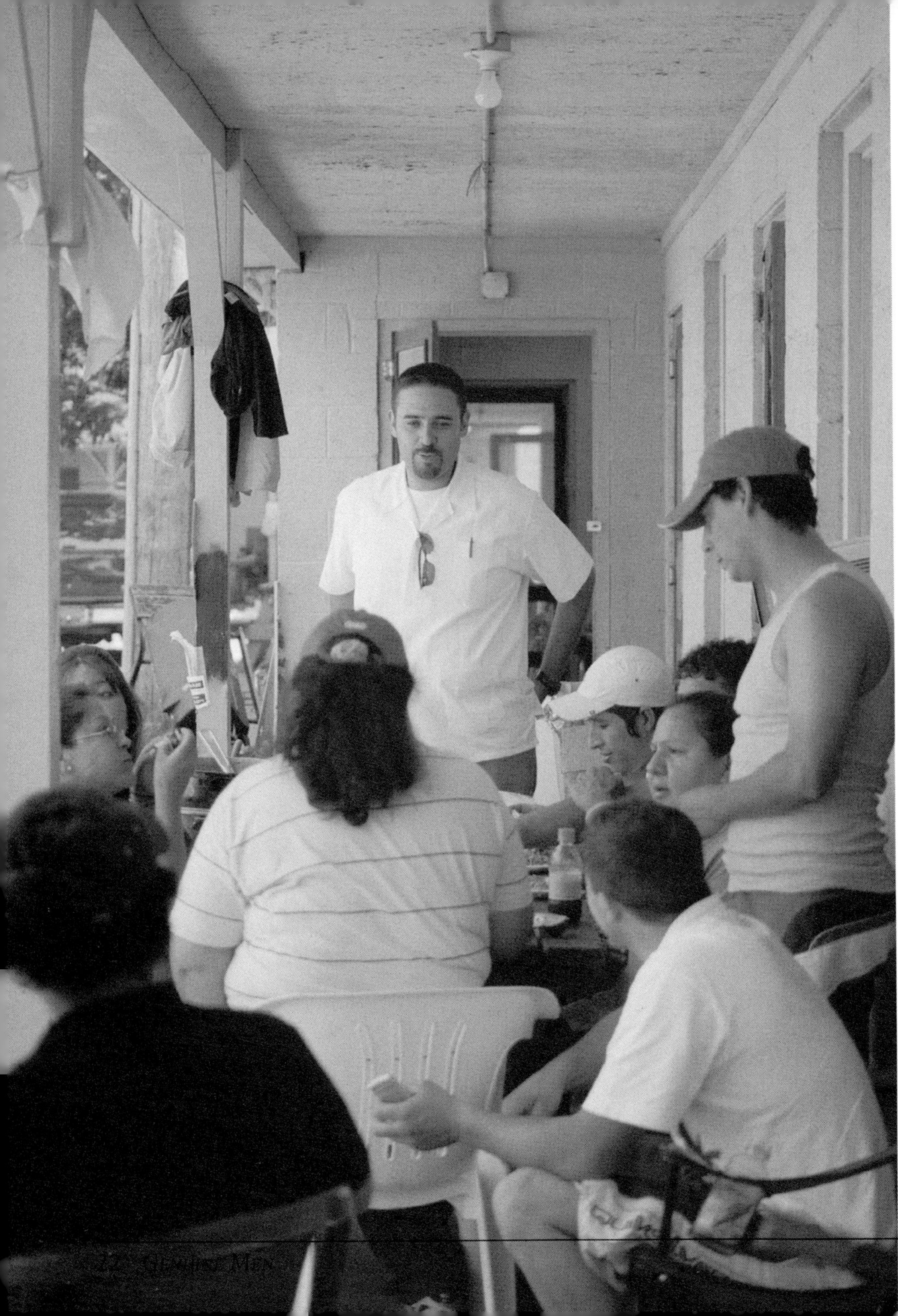

supplies for school, and helping them with their homework. He is their lifeline to a world that does not understand their lives or their struggles.

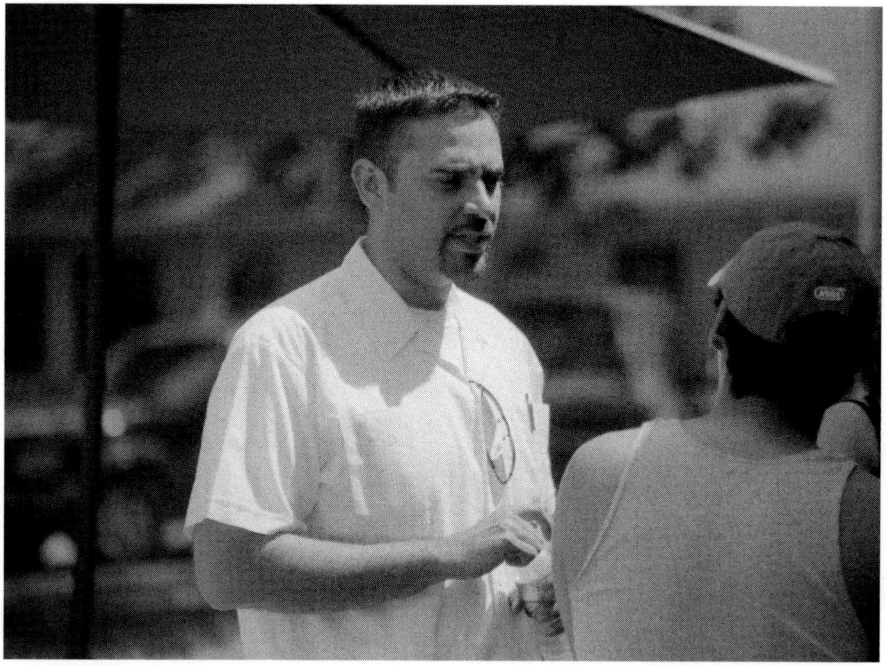

He knows that God has been preparing him for this job his entire life. He studied business management at community college, went on to study at a theology seminary, became a youth minister, and worked in construction for many years. Although he enjoyed the opportunities and comfort that the construction business provided, he always felt deep down that there was another path for him. Today Humberto's life is as complex as it is diverse. Every day he wakes up, he knows that he is going to be called upon to manage a crisis; he never knows what to expect. It is no wonder he keeps a stash of energy drinks. With God by his side, he has learned to use the wisdom the Lord has given him to bring peace and stability to his home and to the homes of others who cross his path as he walks through the backstretch.

Maps, Trees, and Circuits

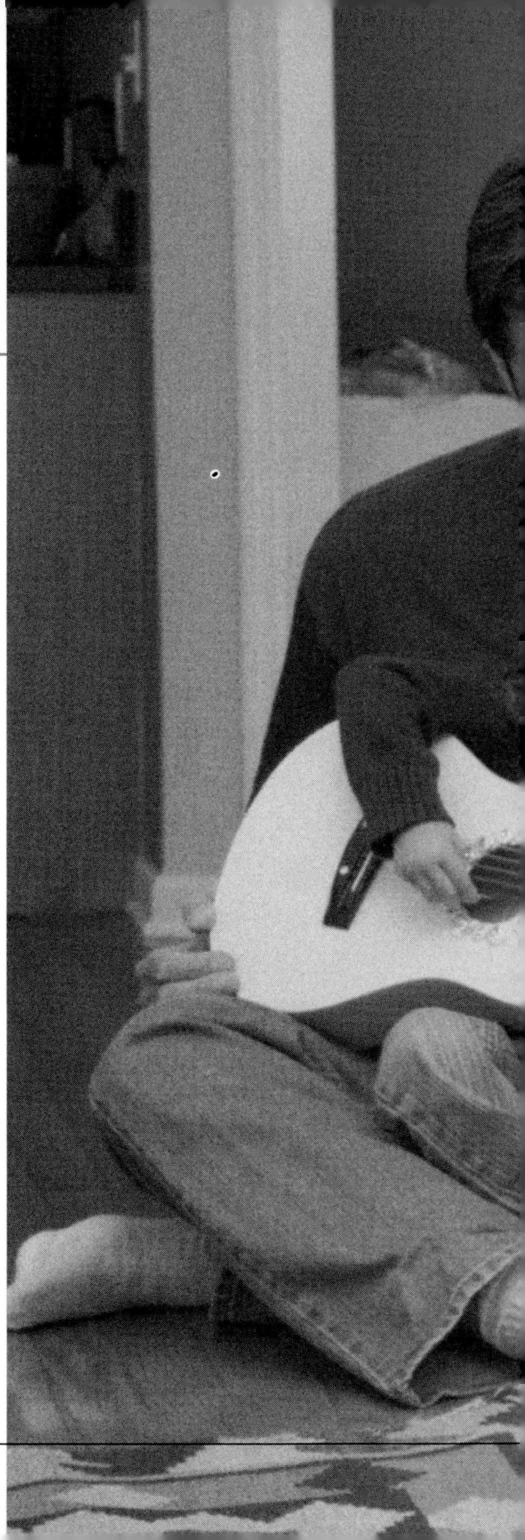

Inspired by his lucky start in life, born to good parents in a quiet part of the world, Oliver believes that it is his responsibility to make the most of the opportunities he's been given. As a kid he thought that it would be fun to be a race car driver—they get to drive so much faster than the cars on the motorways. When he was twelve, he heard that his richest friend's father was a stock broker, and he thought that would be a good choice, even if he had no idea what the man did for a living. At some point he considered having his own business, but he was meant to be an engineer.

More than just a calling, engineering is part of how he is wired as an individual, and it was one of the opportunities presented to him very early in life. His grandfather, a musician by profession, was a self-taught engineer who wrote a book on electronics. His father was also an engineer, and as a child Oliver couldn't think of anyone else in his life who he would rather be like than his father.

Looking back, Oliver felt secure knowing that if everything in the world failed, his father would do whatever was necessary to take care of his family. It wasn't until Oliver transitioned from being his father's son to being his son's father that he truly understood and appreciated what it meant to be responsible for one's self and one's family. Like his father, he does everything in his power to take care of his family.

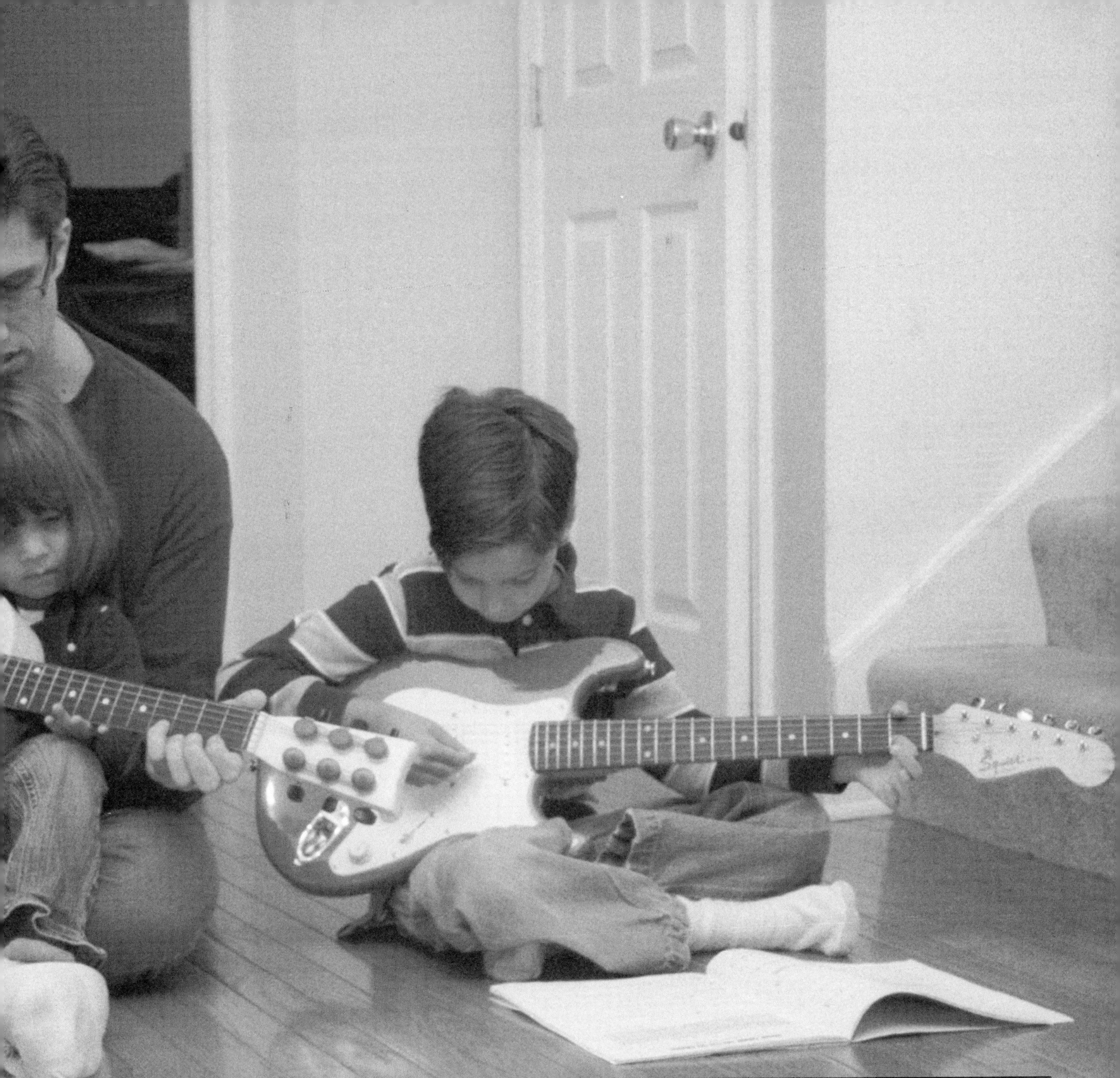

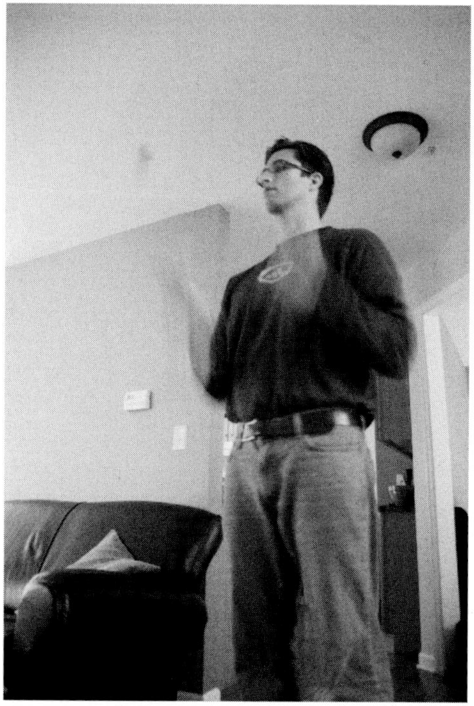

Oliver's approach to life has always been that of a problem solver, never believing that there is just one answer to any problem, but many possible solutions. Oliver uses decision trees—a tool for helping to choose between several courses of action when faced with important decisions. Because he is comfortable with structured decision-making models, every morning Oliver creates a mental map, an overview of the day's terrain. As things change throughout the day, he is equipped to negotiate the twists and turns as they arise.

Decision trees and mental maps help Oliver make informed choices, but it is up to Oliver to translate those decisions into actions. Rather than trying to tackle a situation swiftly and all at one time, Oliver finds that the best way to approach any problem is with persistence, chipping away at it little by little. There is incredible truth in the moral of Aesop's story of the tortoise and the hare: slowly and steadily wins the race. Persistence tells him that, at the end of day, taking just ten minutes out to focus on work, family, and himself will serve him better than never trying—or worse, doing nothing at all.

As an engineer, Oliver is a creator of circuits that he then finds a place for in larger systems. At this point in his life, he is trying to figure out many different things about himself and for himself, including where exactly he fits in the system called life.

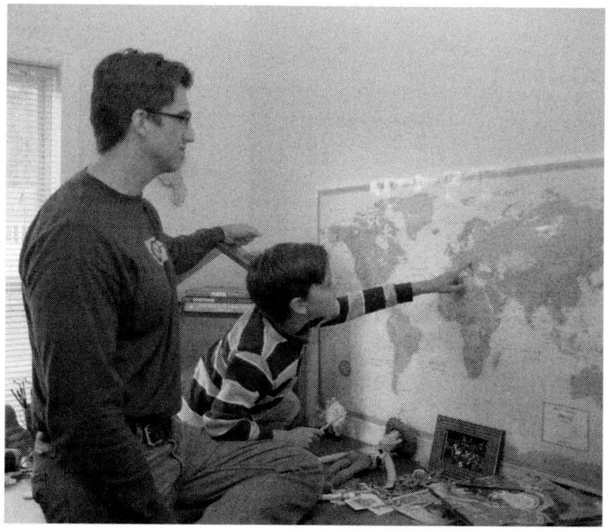

Knowing No Limits

It would have been easier for his mom to place him in a care facility after the accident, but she wouldn't do it. She chose to take on the challenge herself, caring for her son. Yes, the accident took away the use of his legs, but they did not have to accept that as a limitation. She would never give up on James, and she was never going to allow James to give up on himself. His mom believed that he was just like any other child; he just had wheels to help him get around.

James's mother, knowing his physical limitations, explained to him that as long as he mentally applied himself he could do just about anything. James was taught early in life not to argue with his Momma. There were days that kids wouldn't allow him to play because they were afraid that he would roll over them with his chair, but they were also afraid of hurting him. James learned to reassure kids that as long as he knew that he could do something, it was going to be okay.

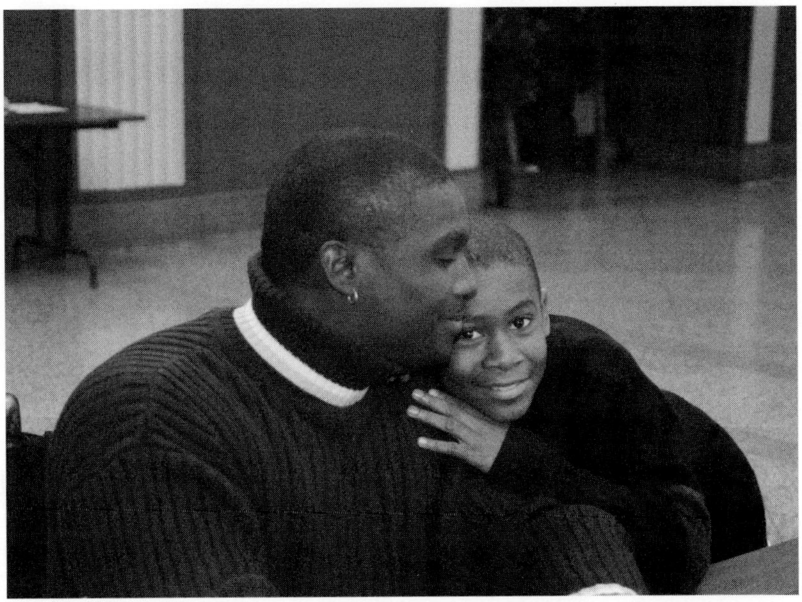

As a teacher and coach, he welcomes questions: can he brush his teeth, go to the bathroom, dress himself, drive a car? Aware that this may be a person's first encounter with someone in a wheelchair, James' answers are like the questions, honest and direct: yes, he can do them all and more. He lives to challenge himself outside the realm of his wheelchair: he lives in a second-floor apartment in a building with no elevator; he is a single dad raising a nine-year-old son; he works with middle school students in an inner-

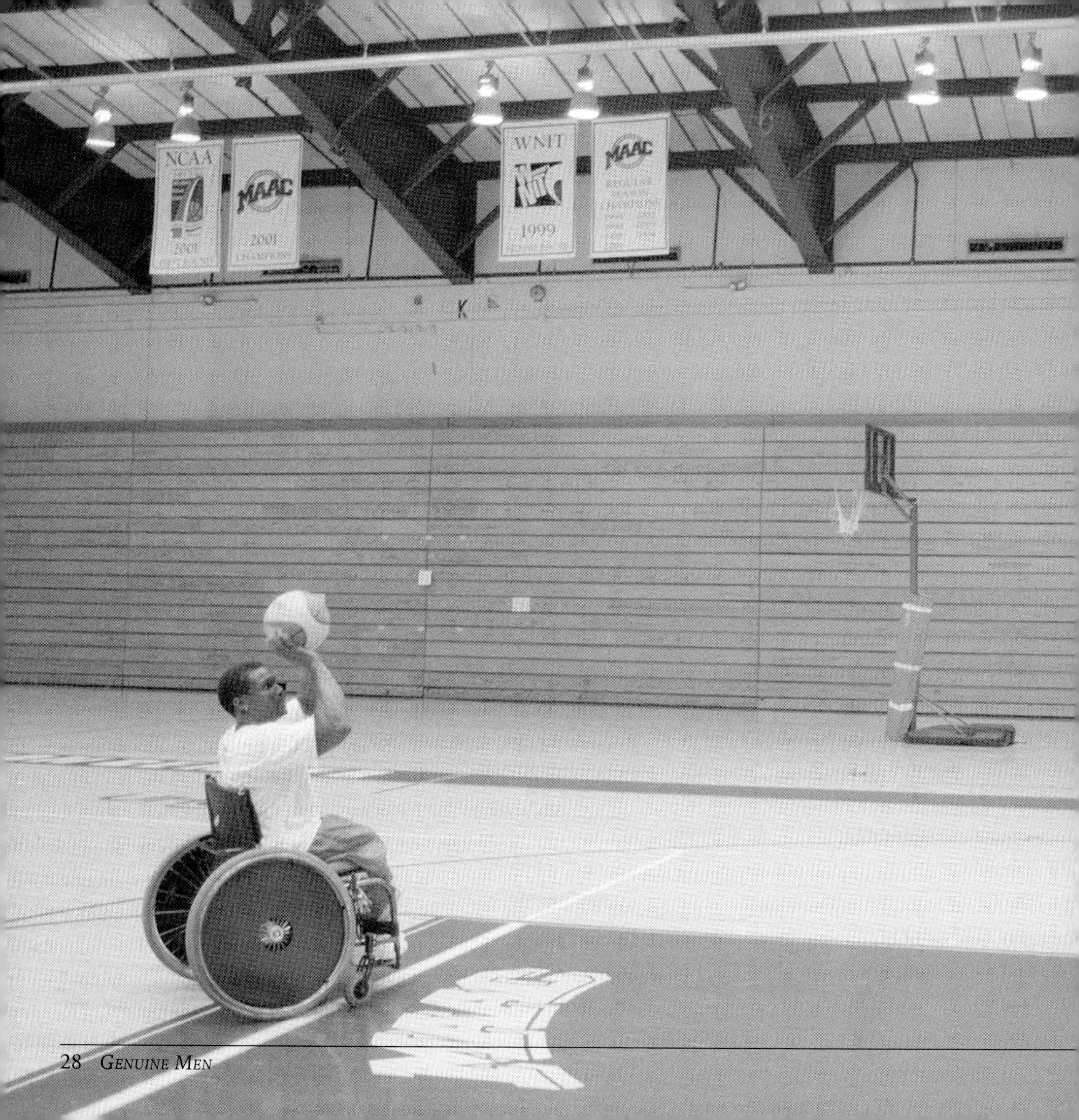
NCAA
2001
MAAC
2001
CHAMPIONS
WNIT
1999
MAAC
REGULAR
SEASON
CHAMPIONS

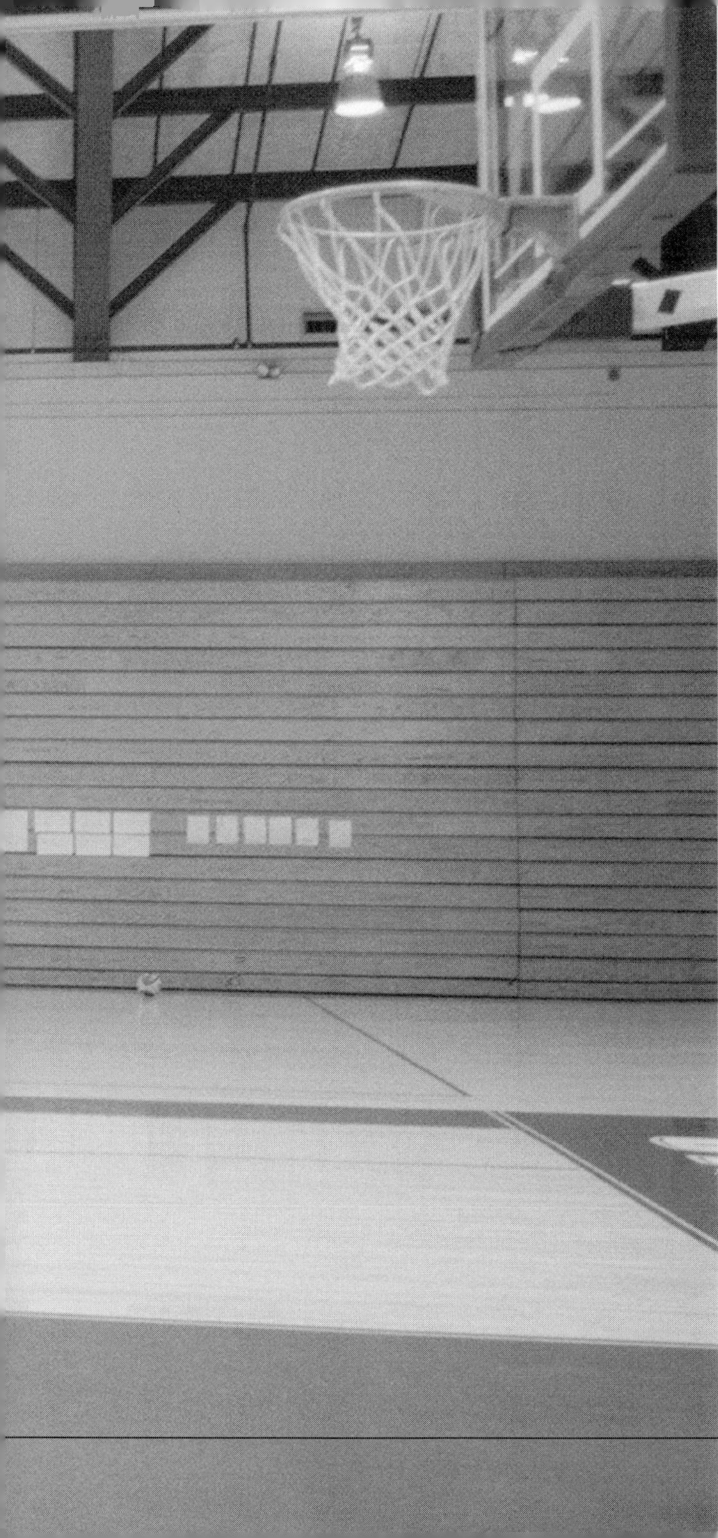

city school; and he is a basketball coach to hundreds of players a year. James has a gift: his wheelchair. It allows him to motivate, advocate, and relate to kids that he may never have been able to affect if he could walk. There are moments he wonders what it would be like to walk, to not always have to work from a wheelchair. But before he completes the thought, he realizes that if that were to happen, he wouldn't be James.

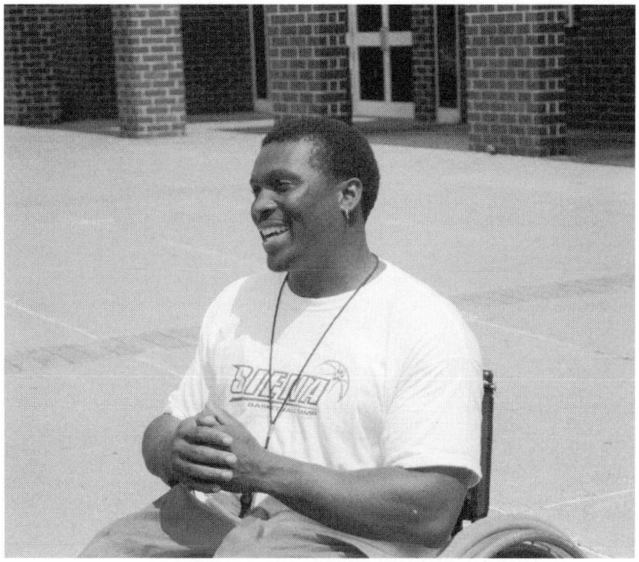

A Businessman's Goals for Life

Mitch learned most of what he knows about life from listening to his grandfather's stories of life in the Old Country and the life he built for himself and his family in his New Country. Though he was a successful businessman in Lithuania, he lost everything in the course of World War II. After surviving the Holocaust, he came with his family to America in 1950 to start a new life. He took a job as a factory worker, earning seventy-five cents an hour. At the age of forty, in the spirit of beginning a new life, he decided that it was time also create a new business.

Mitch was inspired by his grandfather's stories and felt that in his grandfather he had found a kindred spirit. His grandfather taught him that the goals of a business are no different than the goals of a man's life: to achieve independence and self-sufficiency, to provide leadership to those who depend on you for guidance, and to be a contributing member of the community.

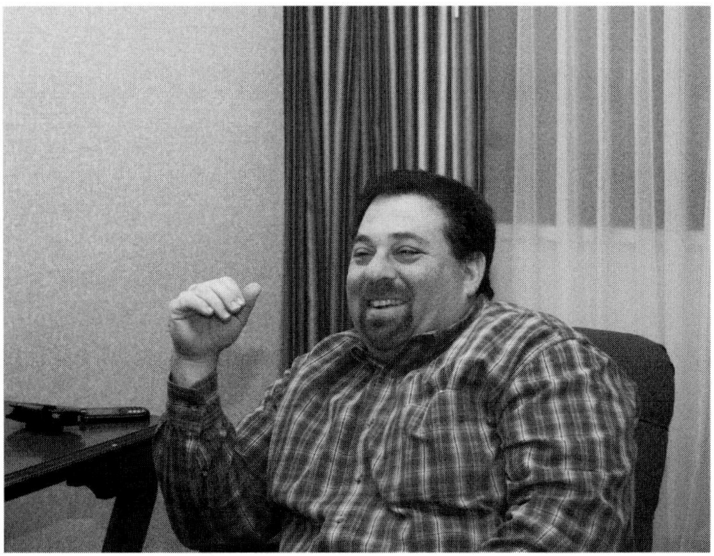

As a young boy Mitch was able to find ways to accomplish whatever goals he set for himself, and he set off to make his own money. Mitch's first business was in the hallways and lunch room at school. He would buy Jolly Ranchers and bubble gum at a local store and sell them for a five- to ten-cent profit. He figured out that by purchasing directly from a candy wholesaler, he would maximize margins and increase his profits. He even learned the art of the deal, selling five pieces of candy for a dollar.

Through high school and college Mitch always had some kind of small venture going, so it was no surprise that he went on to earn an MBA degree. It made perfect sense for him to enter corporate America and put his talents to good use. However, when he got there, Mitch realized that he never lost his entrepreneurial spirit. Mitch had arrived at a crossroads in his career: looking left he saw a position that would put him back in the structure of corporate America, looking right he saw an opportunity to start his own business. Once again, inspired by his grandfather's stories and wisdom, Mitch knew that he was ready to be an entrepreneur and businessman.

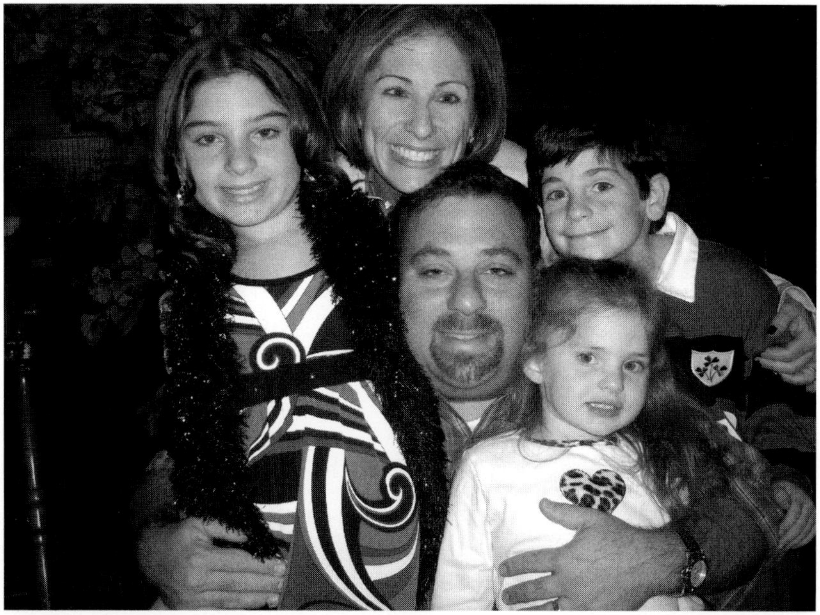

Mitch embraces his entrepreneurial spirit, never losing sight that his business goals are a reflection of who he is as a man: to be independent and self-sufficient, to provide leadership and guidance, and to contribute to his community. Like any good partnership, his marriage is built on common goals he and his wife have set. Together, as Mitch does for his business, they examine complex and difficult issues in order to develop the best solutions for their family. As a parent, the most important thing that Mitch can do for his children is to teach them to be self-sufficient and to encourage them to be independent thinkers and confident decision makers. As a leader in his Jewish community, Mitch shares what he has with others, whether it be helping to secure the financial future of the congregation or teaching Sunday school to the children. Mitch will not deny that he has lofty goals for himself and his business. The way he sees it, as long as he remains true to himself and his beliefs, there is absolutely no reason why he will fail in life or in business.

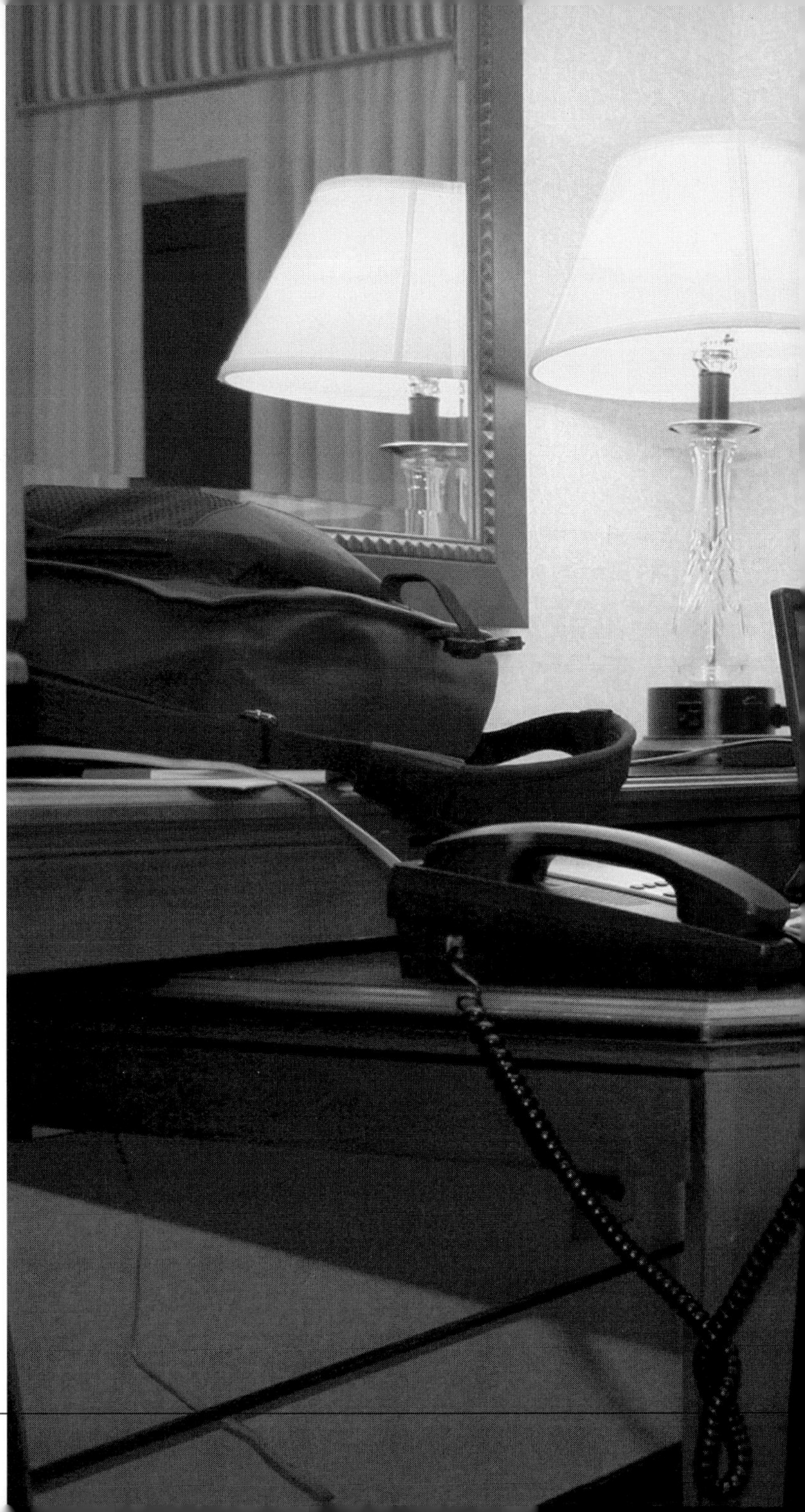

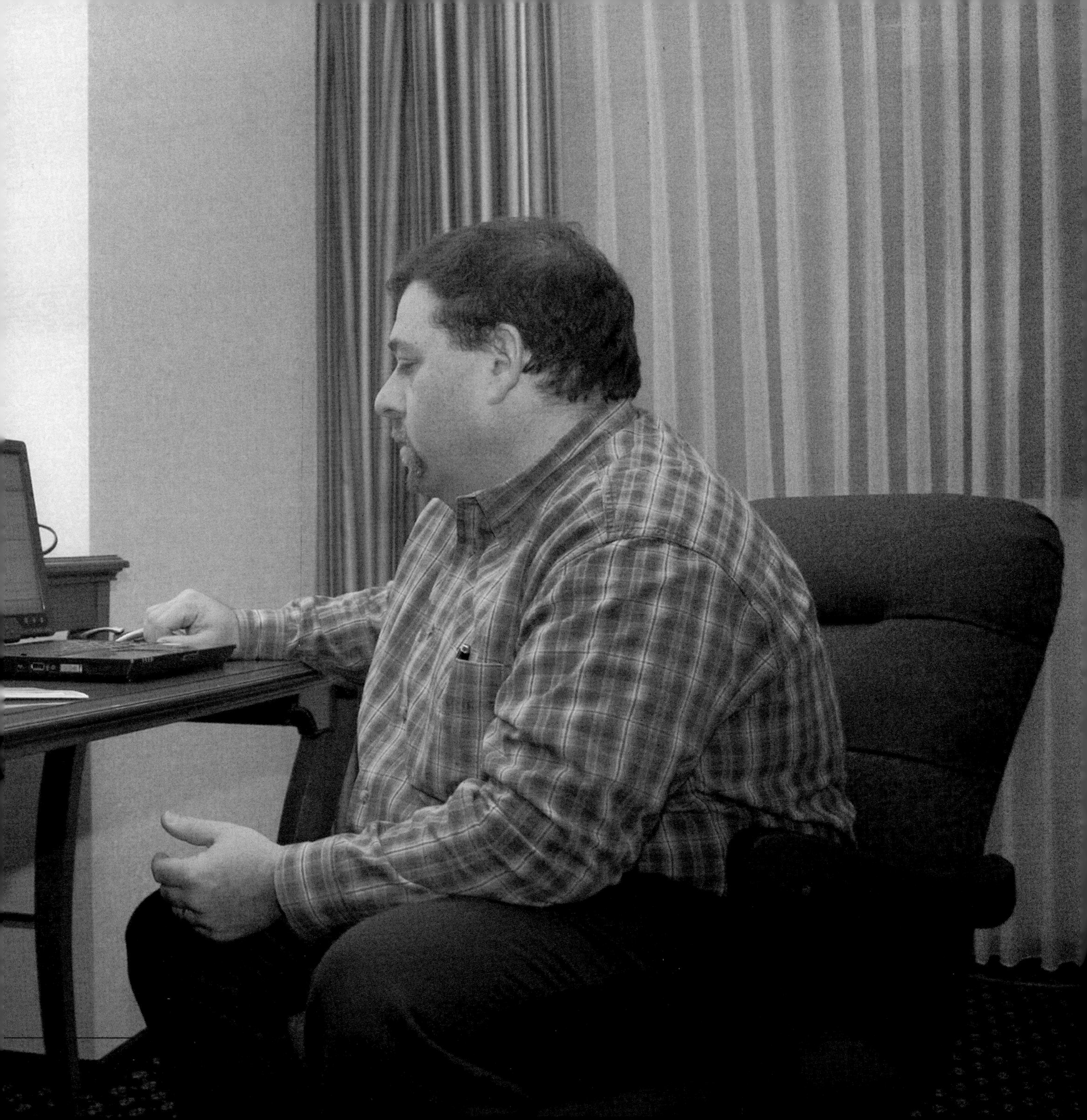

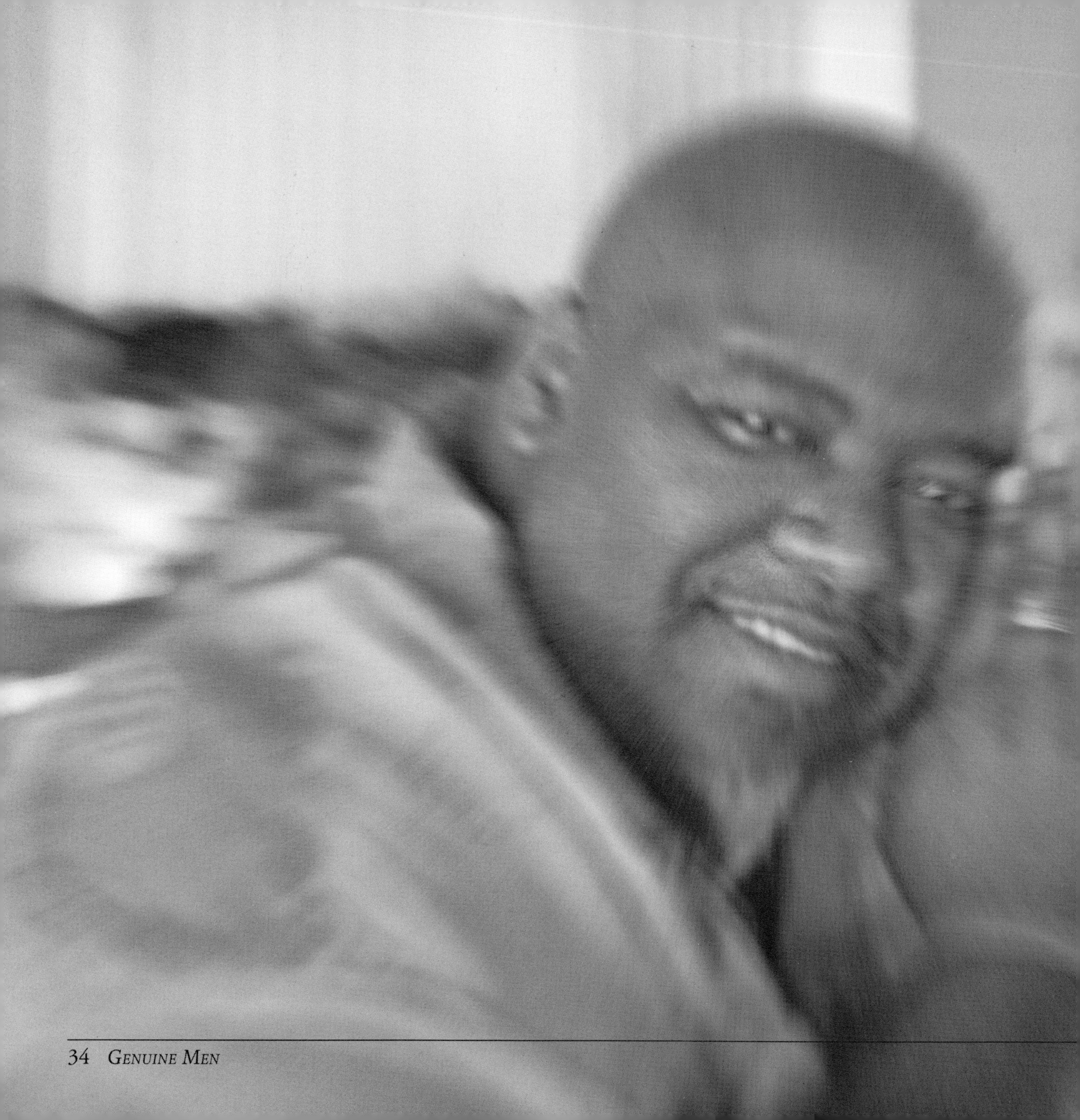

Power of Putting It Out There

Bryant has amazing dreams for himself and his family—dreams that he reaches for each day, dreams that he puts out into the Universe knowing that he has the power to make those dreams reality. As a child, Bryant's mother involved him in the spiritual practice of Nichiren Buddhism. It was not until Bryant was a teenager that he consciously took ownership of the belief that by chanting with confidence in one's innate highest human potential that self-doubt can be dispelled, problems can be challenged courageously, and one's innate wisdom and compassion will be revealed. Encouraged by his youth leader to set life goals, Bryant wrote on a little piece of paper that when he grew up he would have a job doing something that he really loved, that would allow him to travel, and that would make him lots of money. He put that piece of paper next to his altar and, as most teenagers do, never thought about it again. It would be five years before Bryant would come across his list of determinations. Bryant began to chant Nam-Myoho-Renge-Kyo, focusing again on making the determinations become a reality. Things began to happen for Bryant. He went from club promoter to record promoter: every record he worked on was a hit; every city he went to treated him like a star. Bryant loved what he was doing. He was on the road nine months of the year and was promoted to Director of Promotions for a major record label. He had it all, but he became so blinded by fame and fortune that he was no longer putting anything positive out into the Universe. It wouldn't be long before positive things stopped coming his way.

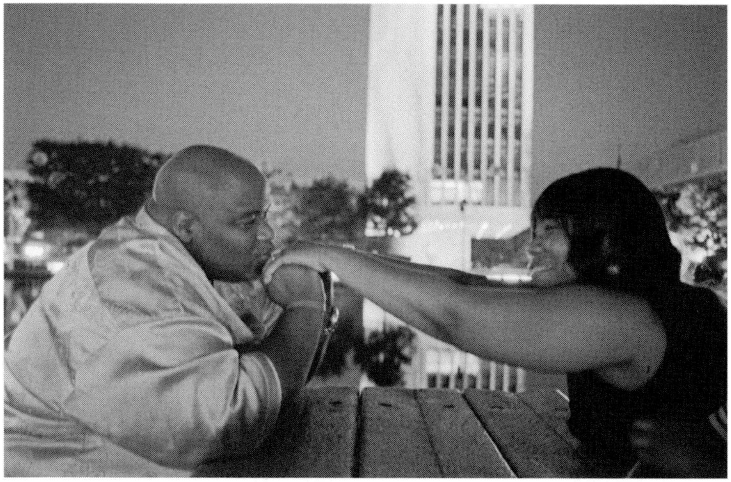

When his life began to unravel, he was almost thirty, alone, and questioning his life. Grasping for a lifeline to help him find his way back to peace and happiness, he reached out to the Buddhist community. With a new set of beads placed in his hands, Bryant began chanting in order to dispel self-doubt, challenge his problems courageously, and have his innate wisdom revealed once again. Thus began the work of creating new determinations to put out to the Universe—what he felt he wanted, and needed at this crossroads. It began slowly: returning to work and then school to earn a degree, meeting a wonderful woman and creating a family, giving back to his spiritual community as a devoted member and leader. It has taken almost a decade for Bryant to rebuild his life. There have been many twists and turns, ups and downs along the way. But because of it all, today he stands very proud of who he is as an individual, and the determinations that he puts forth into the Universe reflect a man who knows the power of putting them out there.

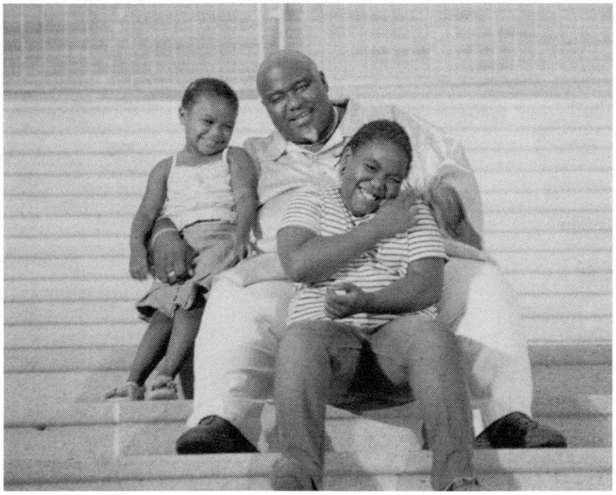

All in the Family

There was nothing better than growing up in a family. His mother welcomed everyone who walked through her front door, and his father loved his children unconditionally regardless of their surname. Walt enjoyed summers on the lake, the chaos that comes with four siblings, and his grandmother, who nurtured and inspired him in the most wonderful ways. His mother chose to give him a strong family name: Walter. Even when kids at school made fun of his name, he didn't care. They never understood how proud Walt was to carry his grandfather's name and make it his own. Not that it mattered; Walt was just like his name: adopted.

He finished high school feeling unfocused, and he left his family to live a bachelor's life. He enjoyed the freedom, but missed the comfort that family always brought to his life. By the time he was twenty, he found himself in the role of husband and father. Walt needed to provide for his family, and the Air Force offered him a way. The military was a new branch on Walt's family tree. It provided his life with basic necessities: food, shelter, education, a support system for his fledgling family, and the possibility of a great future.

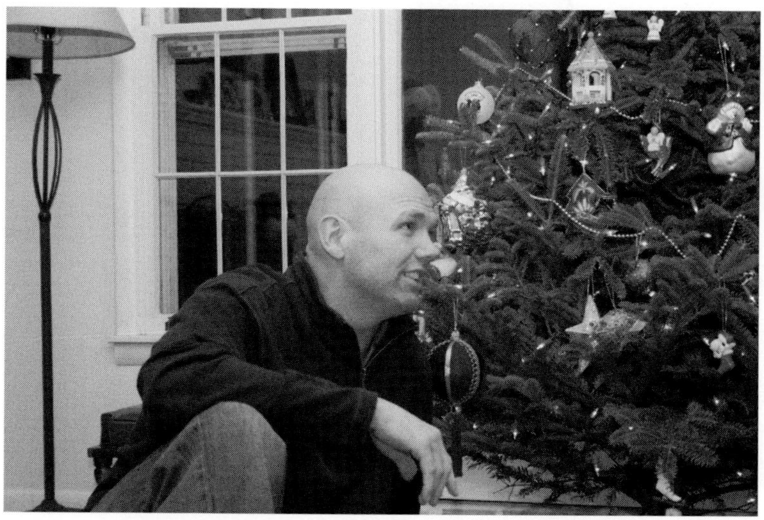

Parental figures within the military instilled in Walt discipline and direction, and helped him understand what it meant to stand up and take responsibility for one's actions. During his early years in the Air Force, Walt matured from a boy to man, a milestone that did not go unnoticed by his grandmother the first time she saw him in his Air Force blues. His wife, child, and career gave him a sense of purpose and being. Walt felt that his life was complete. Three weeks before Christmas, in the cold of North

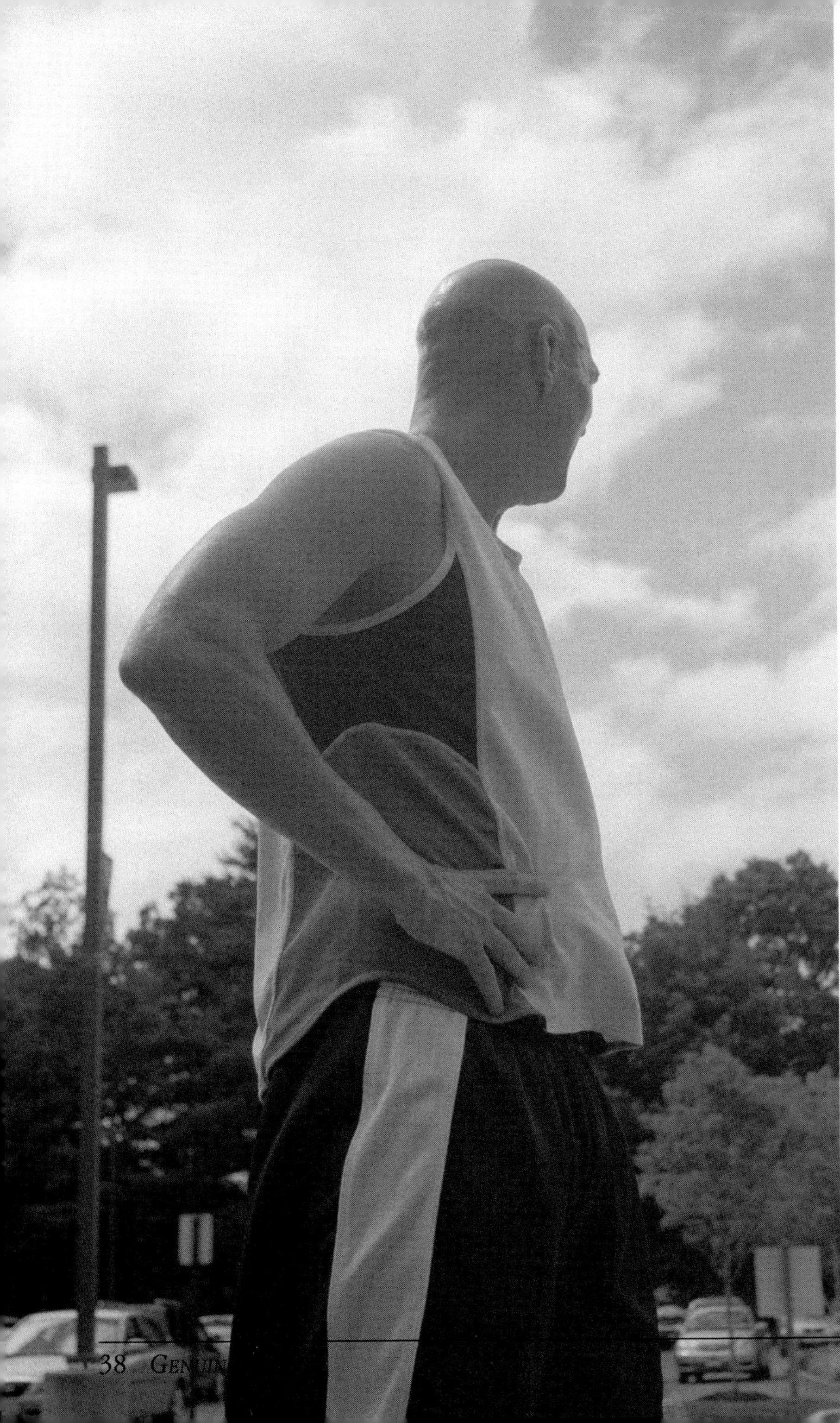

Dakota, he found his baby girl in her crib…gone to be with the angels. Why would God do this? He was forced to consider and reconsider his faith and everything else that he believed in of this world. His grandmother came to him with words of comfort: "Time heals the heart." Perhaps time makes it livable, but there is no getting over a lost child.

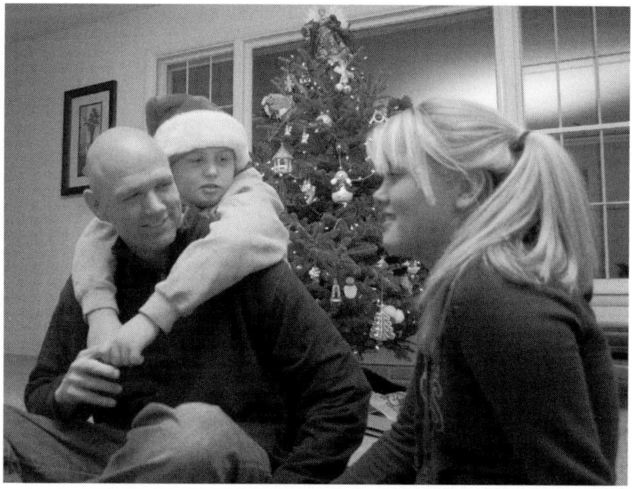

Though he was still a young man, it felt like he had lived a lifetime before the age of thirty-five. He turned again to his grandmother for sage advice; this time it would have to be a memory of them sitting on her porch that would serve him: "The world owes you no living. You work for or earn everything you have." Walt knew in his heart that there was so much out there for him to live for, especially his family. Walt began by working on his life moment by moment, then day by day, and eventually the days became months that turned into a year.

When he chose to leave the brotherhood of the Air Force, he found himself no longer surrounded by men with whom he felt he shared common interests and experiences. To fill this void in his life, he created a new branch on his family tree, comprised of other men who supported him, inspired him, and motivated him because of what they had done in their own lives. He no longer feels like a lonely soul on some remote, untraveled road. Today, there are so many things that he wants to do: run the Boston Marathon, travel across the country, visit exotic ports, bungee jump…create another new branch on his family tree. Knowing that his life is far from complete, he is just finding comfort and a new level of peace. With his kids by his side and an angel on his back, Walt continues to move forward through life.

The Way It Is Supposed to Be

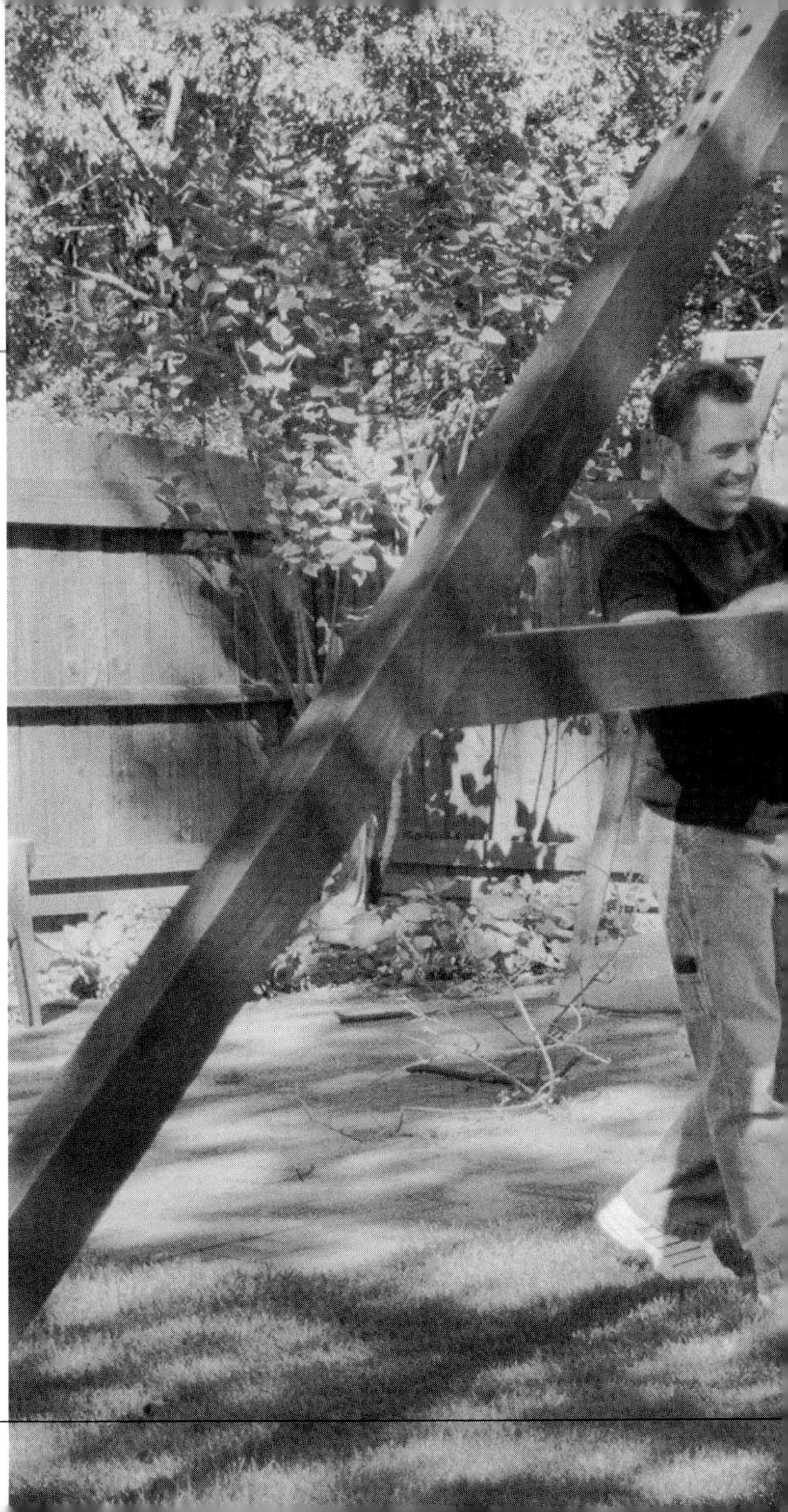

His favorite song begins by asking the question, "Who is to say what is impossible?" As a shy and nervous kid growing up, he followed his dad around just to get a shot at fixing things with him. His dad worked hard because it meant a better life for his family. Rob was the first from his family to attend college, and as his mind began to spread its wings, there was no stopping his curiosity. Young, ambitious, and driven to succeed, Rob was burning the candle at both ends professionally and personally. A businessman Rob liked and respected took him under his wing and shared with him a hard-earned lesson: In life and business, when an opportunity presents itself, no matter how great it may appear, far more success will be gained if it is approached calmly, objectively, and from every angle. You risk ending up with a lot less than you deserve if you leap too quickly.

Heeding his mentor's words, Rob took advantage of opportunities that presented

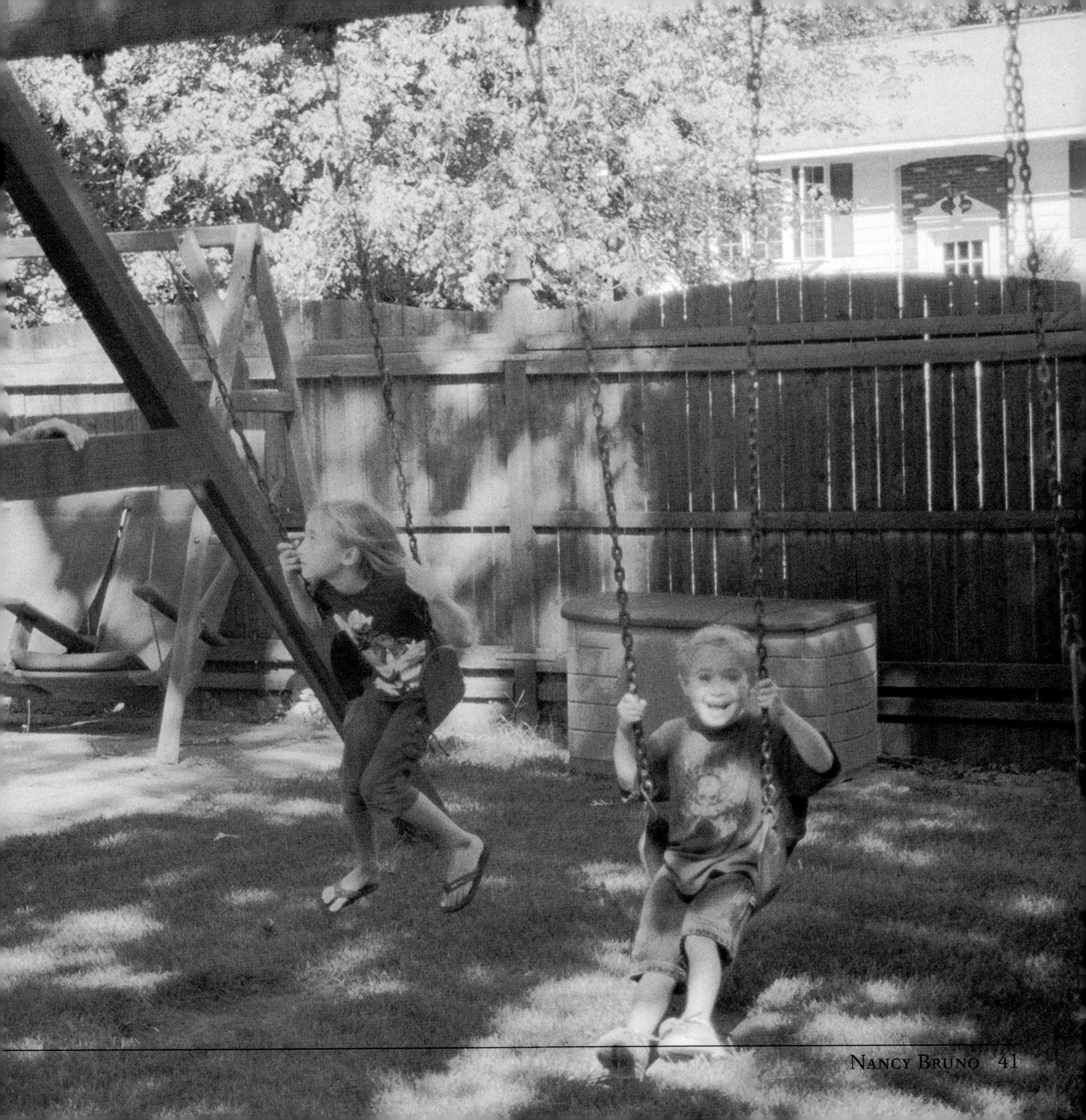

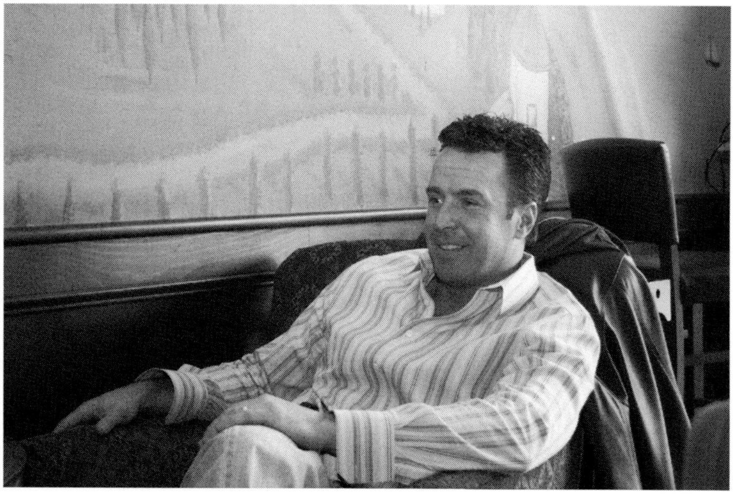

themselves as stepping-stones to the life he envisioned for himself and his family. His parents were curious about his choices and decisions—they were so different from their own. However, their skepticism became Rob's motivation to succeed; it was a driving force that to this day keeps him striving for more, working harder, solving complex problems, and taking on new challenges. There is a pull inside of him to always be doing something: clients to please, meetings to take, school events to attend, projects to be completed at home. Striking a balance between work and family is difficult, but as a parent he tries to instill in his children the importance of working for what they want in their lives.

At this stage of his life he wants to provide for his family and be a presence in their lives; he is finding ways to make this happen. He is motivated by the series of moments that make up his life: his parents cheering for him at one of his little league games, watching his future wife walk down the aisle toward him on their wedding day, walking into what would become his family's home for the first time, driving his new Mercedes to his parent's house, the birth of his children, the first unsolicited "I love you" from each of his children, having a catch with his son, watching his daughter ride a horse. During each of these moments he paused and gave each the respect they deserved. Yes, it is important to work hard and overcome the impossible, but it is equally important to drink in the moments of his life. With each new day that passes he feels a change in everything, and he knows that this is how it is supposed to be for him.

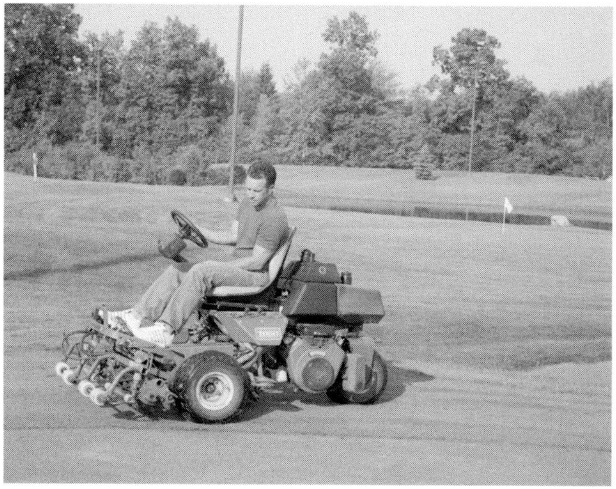

Returning the Gift

From the beginning, the odds were not in his favor. Patrick was a child of a child; he was born when his mother was just seventeen. His father was never in the picture. To this day he is inspired by her struggle. She is the strongest woman he has ever met in his life. The road they traveled was not smoothly paved; it was dusty, rocky, and full of curves and detours. Yet, despite what sometimes felt like a hopeless lot in life, he always remembered that there were people in the world who had it worse than his family. With that in mind, Patrick pledged that he would take the gifts that God gave him and return them to others.

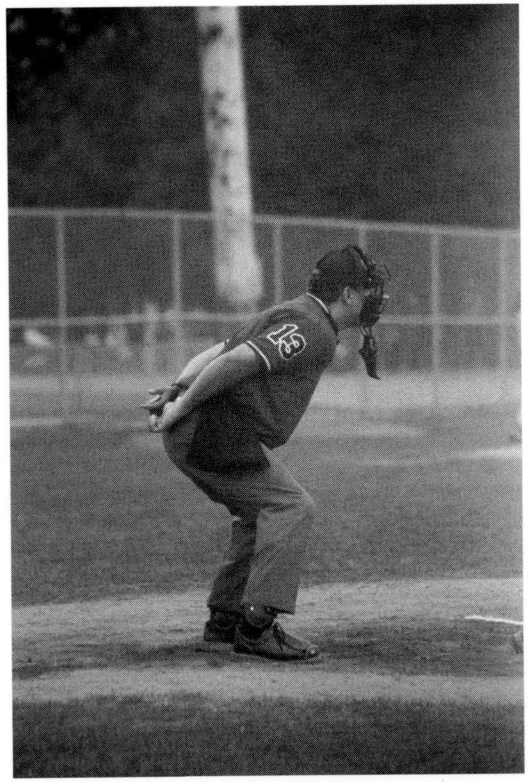

The first true gift he received was the gift of baseball. He was a depressed and anxiety-ridden child, and his happiest childhood memory is the day he met a boy named Jeff. Jeff saw Patrick walking alone down the sidewalk, and he took him behind the Polish Community Center and taught him how to play baseball. It was a break Patrick never asked for or anticipated but desperately needed. Through baseball he made lifelong friends, discovered a lifelong passion, and found happiness. Never forgetting what the game of baseball did for him, Patrick volunteers as a coach, and his mission is to teach his players to respect the game, develop good skills, and always have a good time.

The next gifts he received were the gifts of education and ice cream. When it was time to attend college he truly had no idea what he wanted to study. He only knew that he never wanted to be in a position where he couldn't care for his family. College was the only avenue toward that life. In time, he found his niche, and

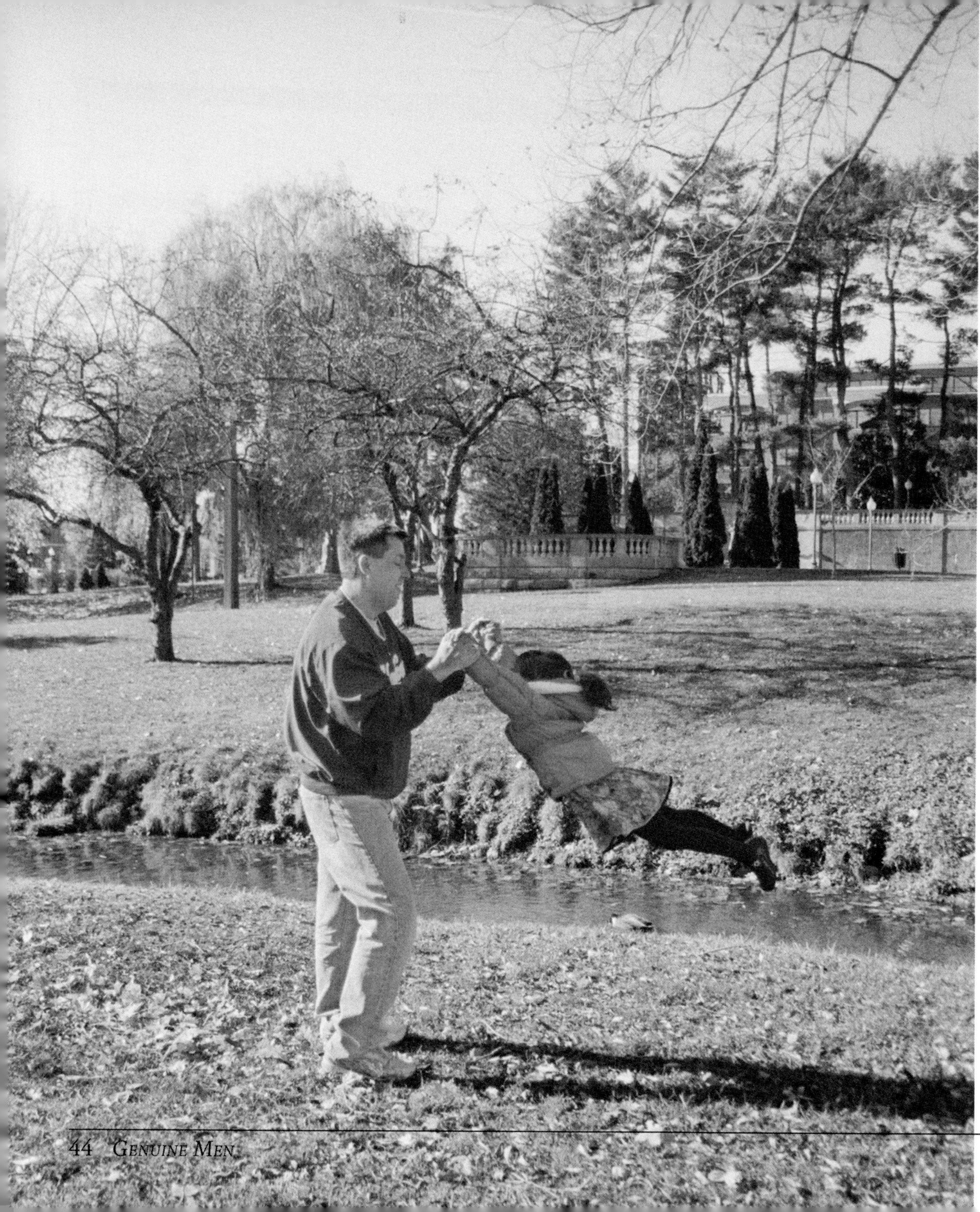

the proudest moment of his life was the day he graduated with his bachelor's degree. He began his career in hotel management but was soon offered a position as manager for a successful ice cream business. The owners saw promise and drive in this young man; they knew they could entrust their business to Patrick. Although he loved his job, he knew that he wanted more for himself. He decided to return to college and earn an MBA. After he had his business degree in hand, the owners came to Patrick with an offer he couldn't refuse: to own his own business. He works hard, travels quite a bit during the summers, and the days can be very long, but he wouldn't have it any other way. Owning his own business allows him to live life on the terms he chooses and entrenches him in his community. A scoop of ice cream can make tears go away, soothe a sore throat, act as a reward for a good report card, turn around a bad day, be the reason for a first date, or ease a breakup. It is a true gift to pass across the counter.

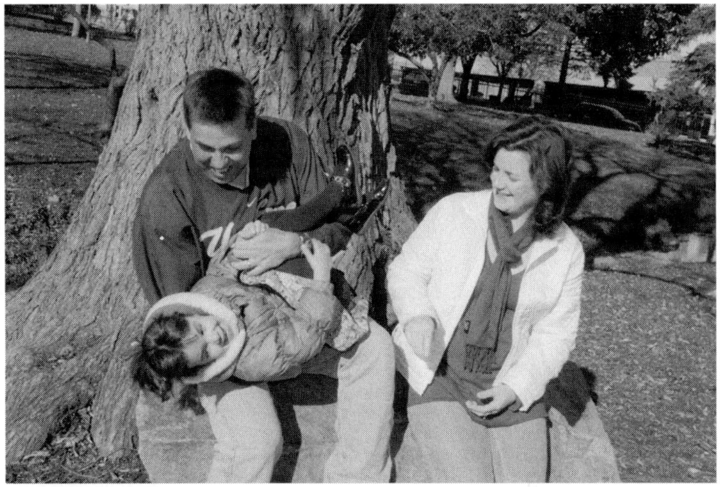

At the end of each day Patrick takes a moment and asks himself, "Did I do something for my marriage to make it better today? Did I do something to make my family and friends better off or healthier today? Did I do something to make my store and staff stronger today? Did I do something for my community at large today?" He is neither a saint nor is he Santa Claus, just a man trying do all he can, in every way that he can, for as many people as he can, for as long as he can.

MASTERING SELF

For Stephen, the question within has always been, who is he? His identity was determined by an oppressive Southern culture system put into practice generations before he was born. His father was Cherokee Indian and his mother was African American and Native American. Both were automatically classified as black Americans by Southerners. His parents constantly reinforced that he should not allow anyone or anything to limit the vision he held for himself, but it was hard as a kid to stand up against the crowd. Stephen dealt with the inequality in his community by learning to adjust to those around him so *they* felt comfortable in his presence. This coping strategy made day-to-day life easier, while also earning him friends, but early on it never really helped him to stand up for the fact that he was much more than the color of his skin. That would come later.

Despite accomplishments as an athlete and student, artist and dancer, husband and

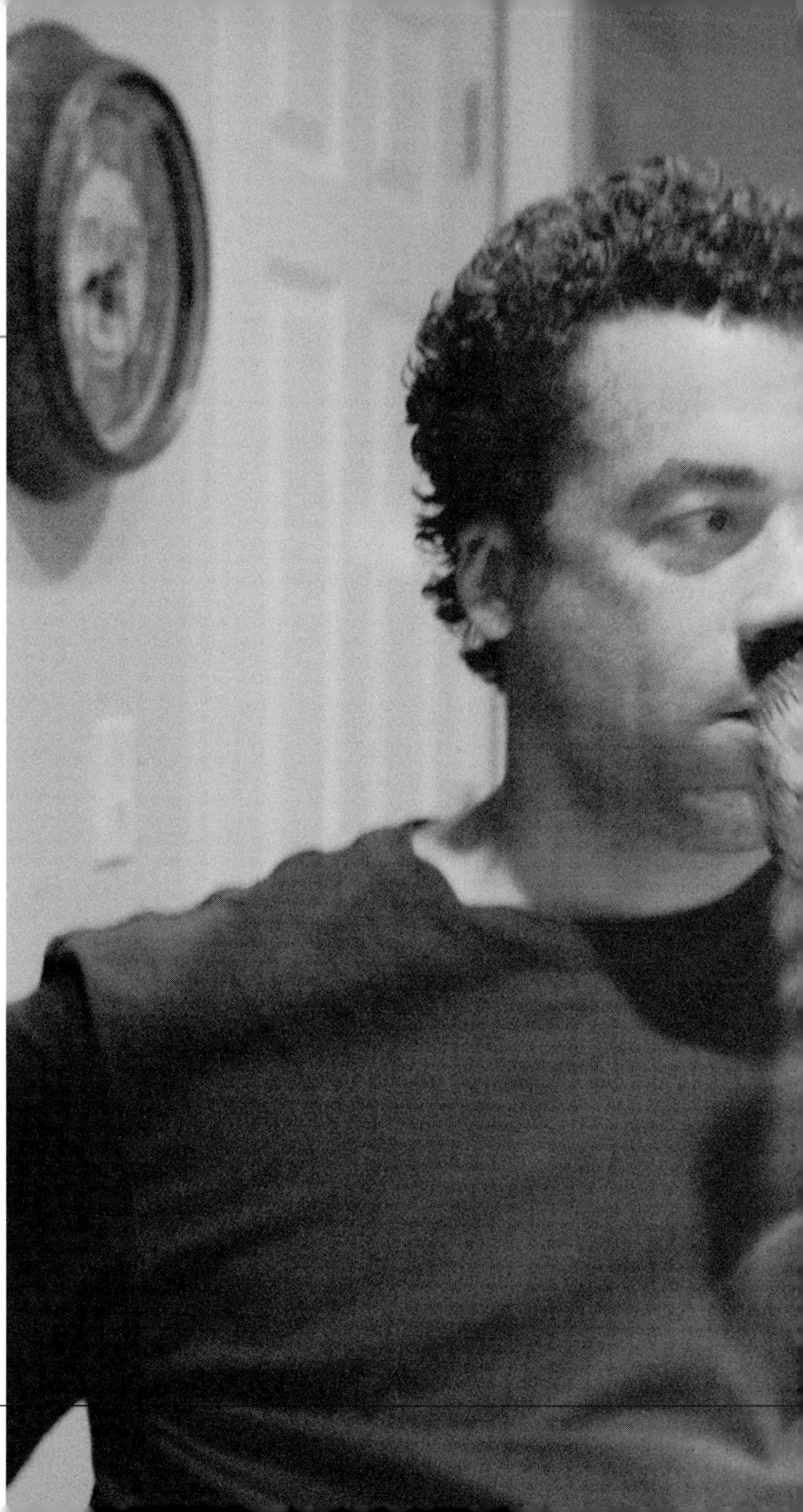

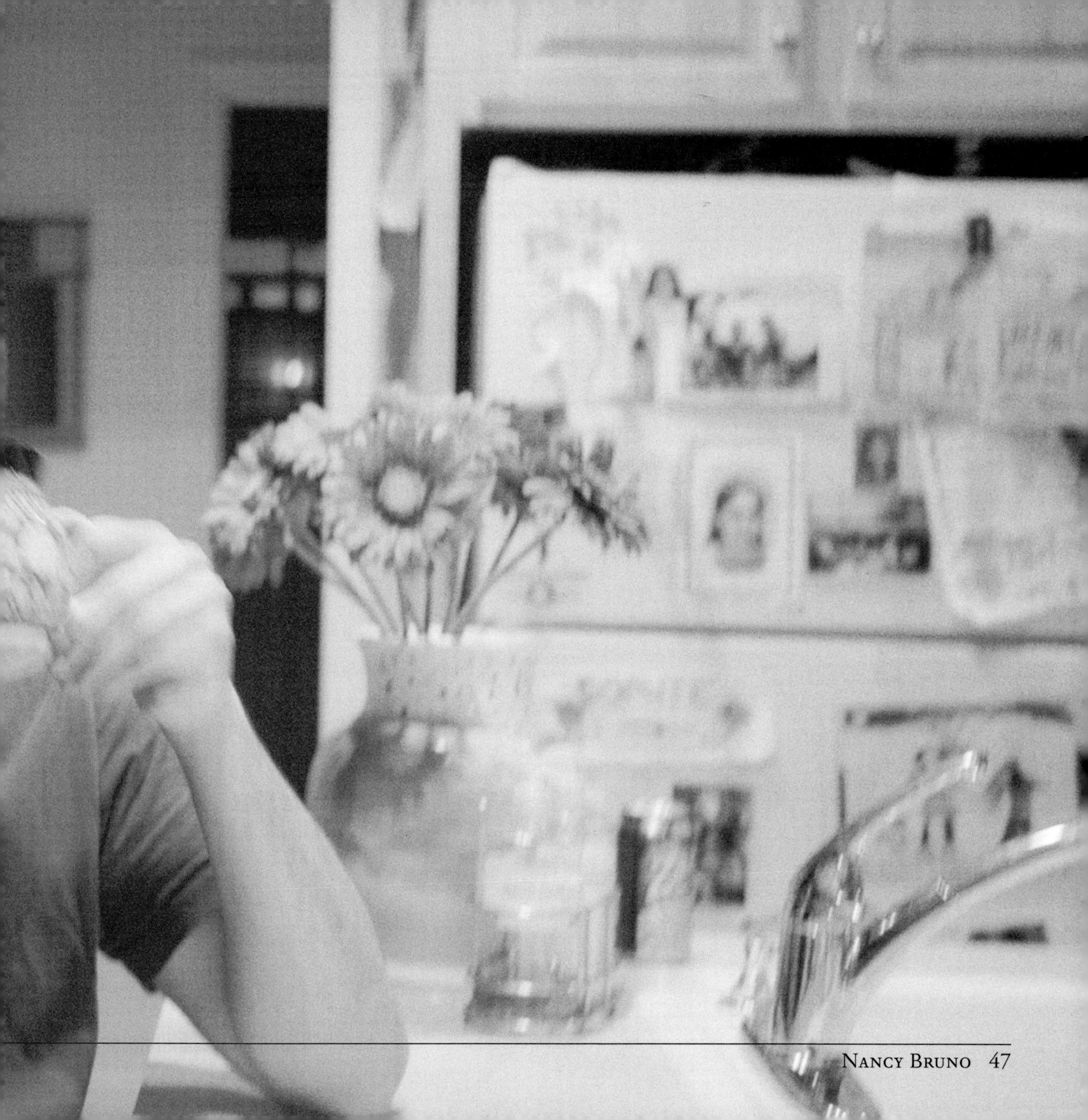

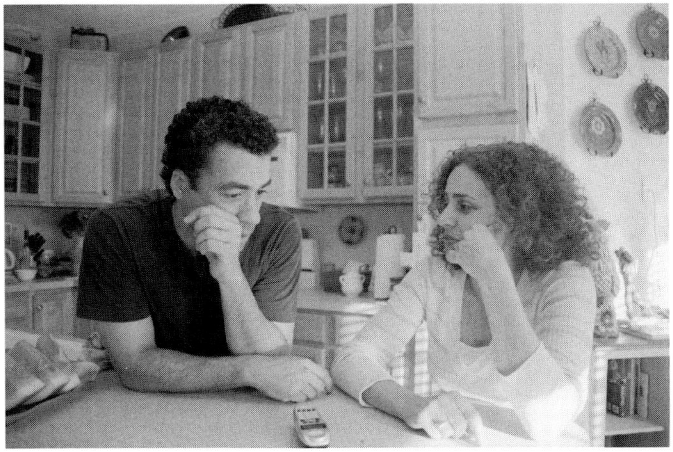

father, entrepreneur and respected member of the community, he was moving from one thing to the next waiting to find…himself. A cousin, recognizing his inner struggle, asked him a life-changing question: "What are you going to do with *your* life?" He was called to task. He could no longer deny that what he was up against was bigger than a man trying to find a purpose. He was, and had been for over twenty years, battling depression. It was time to move away from the darkness and head into the light. It began by making two very important and personal decisions: he was not going to take medication, and he was going to document the entire process. For Stephen it was not about simply covering up the darkness, but getting rid of what was at the core of his depression. Slowly, he began shedding the layers of his history, the negative beliefs and thought patterns that others forced upon him, but that he chose to carry. Each day was like a single grain of sand shifting across a scale, until one day the scale finally tipped in his favor.

Moving forward is an ongoing process that doesn't stop just because he feels better. It's a challenge to manage all of the little moving parts that permit him to choose happiness, and there are days he can feel himself slipping a bit. In these moments he turns toward the people he considers masters in their own right, the ones he knows will provide him with sage advice: his mother, who pushes him to always be his best example of himself, for himself and others to experience; his compassionate and steady wife, who only ever saw the best in him because she only operates in the light; his older brother, who accepts himself for his flaws and greets criticism with a thank you; his sister, who is a true example of faith and determination; and his dear friend and father figure, who is a master of himself and human nature. Stephen listens to their positive messages, absorbs their wisdom, and makes it his own. Stephen has mastered his past and now passes on to his children—and one day to his grandchildren—his true story, beliefs, and spirit.

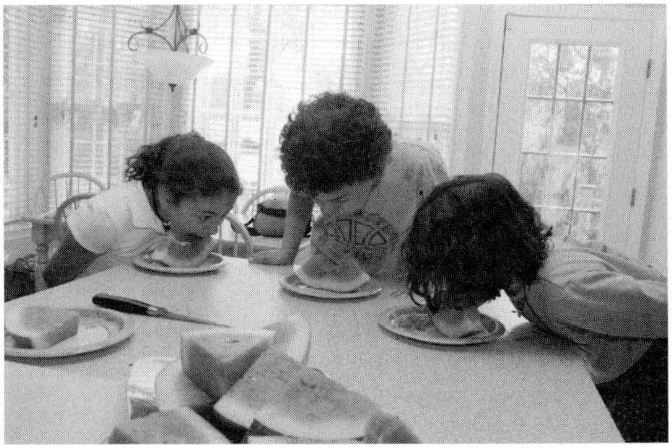

Road to Manhood

There comes a time in every boy's life when he looks his dad in the eye and they both know that it is time for the boy to begin his journey toward being his *own* man. It is in that moment of realization that both father and son must acknowledge that the boy will make choices that are *unlike* the choices of his father. Joey and his father had their moment when Joey was around twelve years old. Growing up, hunting and fishing were rites of passage, where skills and stories were passed down through the generations. It was not something that always sat well with Joey, but he rose to the occasion of being his father's son. The day Joey shot and killed his first animal, everything changed. Immediately, he knew that outdoorsmanship was not for him, and he had to tell his father. What made it difficult was knowing that his choice would not meet with approval from those with whom he had always been the closest, and this was the first time he was going to stand on his own without a safety net. Knowing in his heart that he was doing what was right for him, Joey found the strength and courage to express his conviction to no longer hunt or fish. Standing up to his father in this manner was the first of many steps down the uncharted road toward manhood. There were setbacks and forks in the road where he chose to go left when going right *may* have been the better option by others' standards, but none of that mattered because Joey realized that he was traveling the road of his life: finding his likes and dislikes, forming his own ideas, and making his own mistakes.

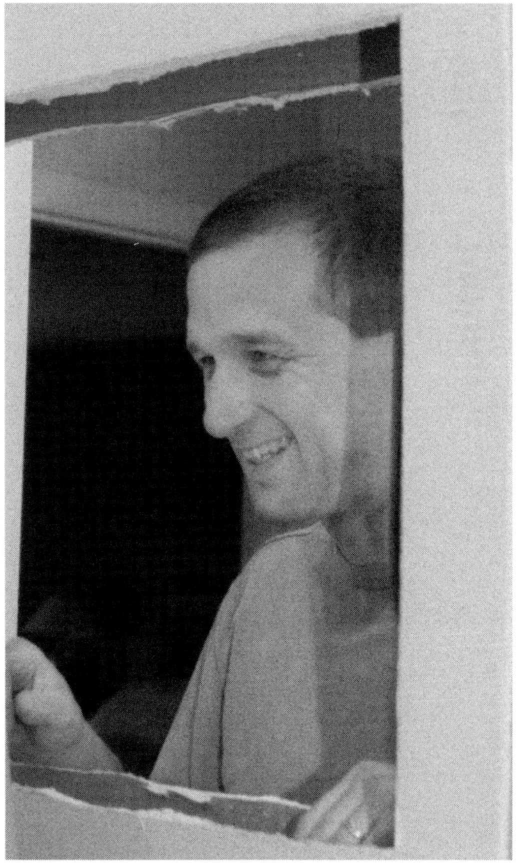

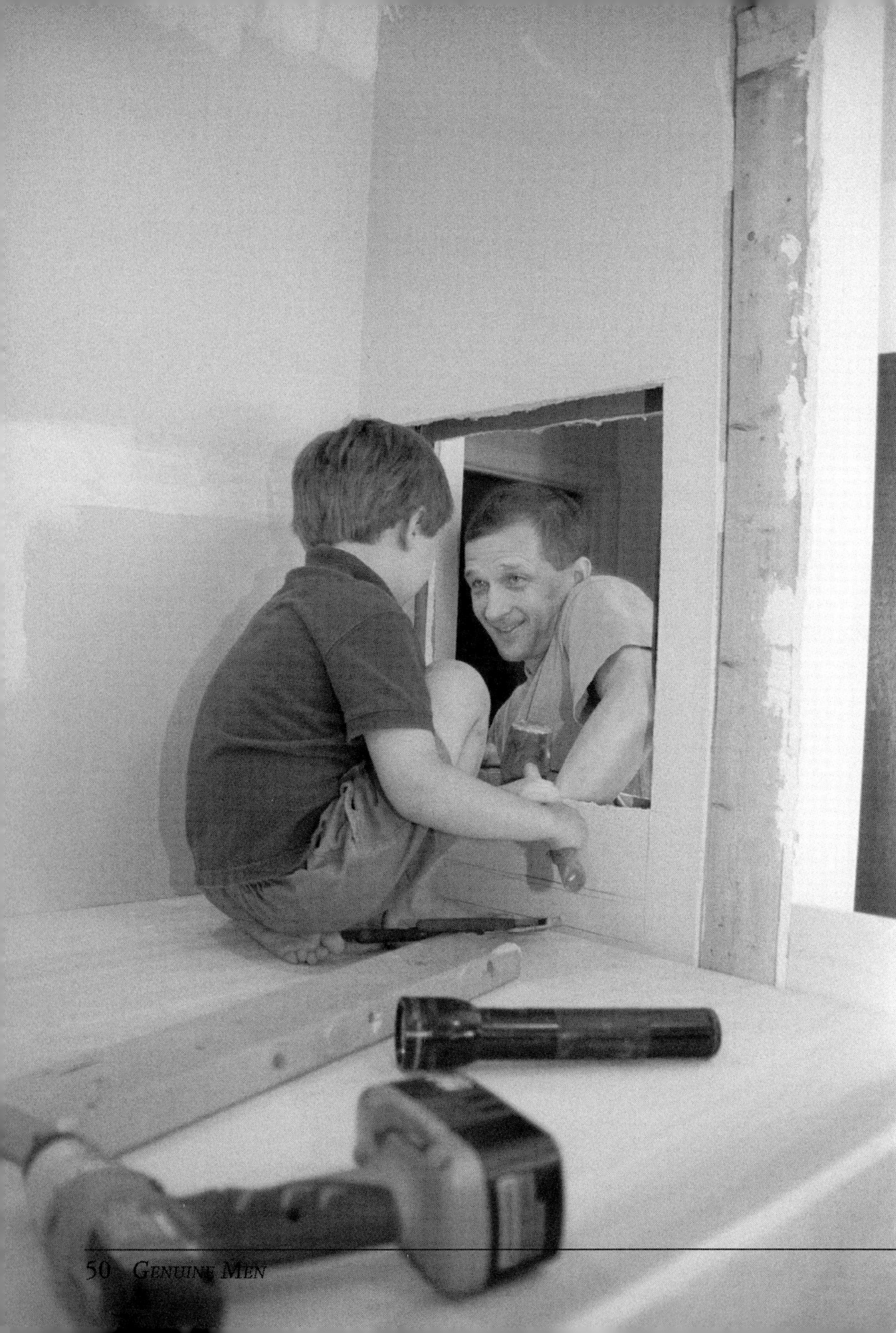

He thought perhaps now he knew what it was to be a man, but at twenty with no responsibilities and little direction, he had no idea what it meant to be a man. What brought everything together for Joey was the unconditional love of a woman who guided and grounded him when he needed focus and provided a haven that allowed him the opportunity to spread his wings and soar as he had never before in his life. Because of her he was able to find the man inside himself that he had been searching for all of those years.

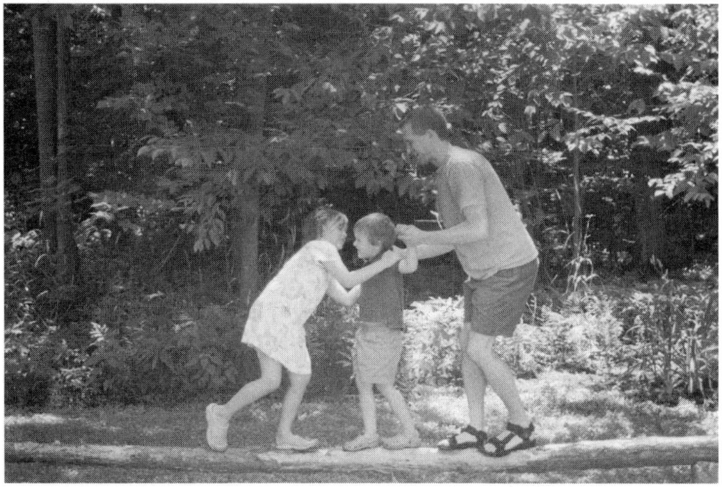

With time, Joey found what he believes to be his true purpose in life: teaching. As an elementary school teacher he stands out as one of the few male teachers, but he does not stand unsupported or alone in his tight-knit community. He has learned through his own experiences that there is space for mutual respect for all lifestyle choices. And with that, when he looks at his son and sees his reflection in the young boy's eyes, he knows that one day when they least expect it, their eyes will meet and they will both know that it is his son's time to follow the road to being a man.

FAITH

Jimmy was raised in a home filled with the positive energies of love and affection. His parents, both Italian Catholics, made sure Jimmy was baptized, received communion, and was confirmed in the Catholic tradition. However, after his confirmation, Jimmy began questioning whether or not he truly believed in God. By the time Jimmy turned fifteen he declared himself an atheist. Strangely, during the next few years, thoughts of death plagued his mind during the day and his dreams at night. It was then that he decided, without telling a soul, that he would revisit religion.

Rededicated to Christianity, he attended mass during all forty days of the next Lent— again, never telling a soul. His search continued through college with nightly prayer and frequent visits to Church. He met young Franciscan brothers who helped rid Jimmy of the belief that religion was solely about suffering. They helped him discover the gift all Christians have deep inside: the gift of the power of the Resurrection through Faith. Realizing the importance of God and faith was easy compared to making them a priority. There were so many other things that seemed to take a greater or more immediate precedent in his life, faith and God would just get lost in the shuffle. And every time this happened, each time he forgot his beliefs and allowed himself to approach life with a negative view, he suffered greatly. His marriage failed, his business neared bankruptcy, he encountered death, and he lost the true love of his life. Reflecting back upon all of these events, he sees that they were not a string of random acts of bad luck, but a direct result of forgetting the lessons of his true religion: positive energy and

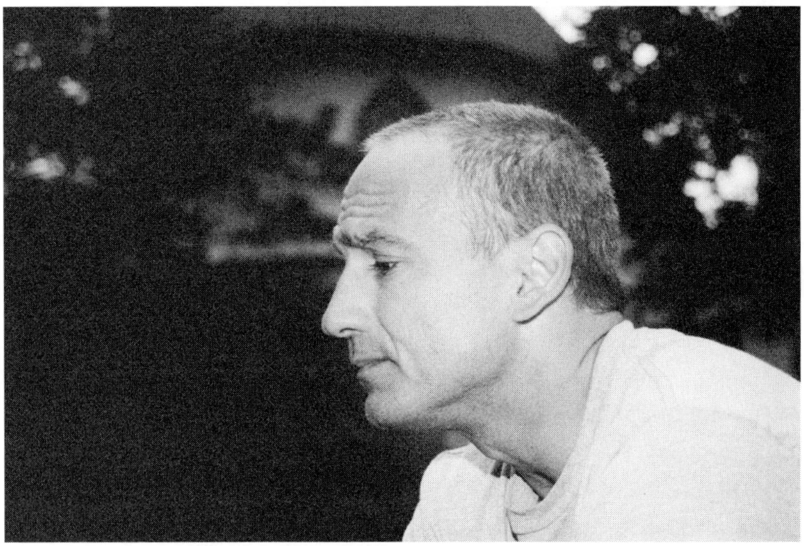

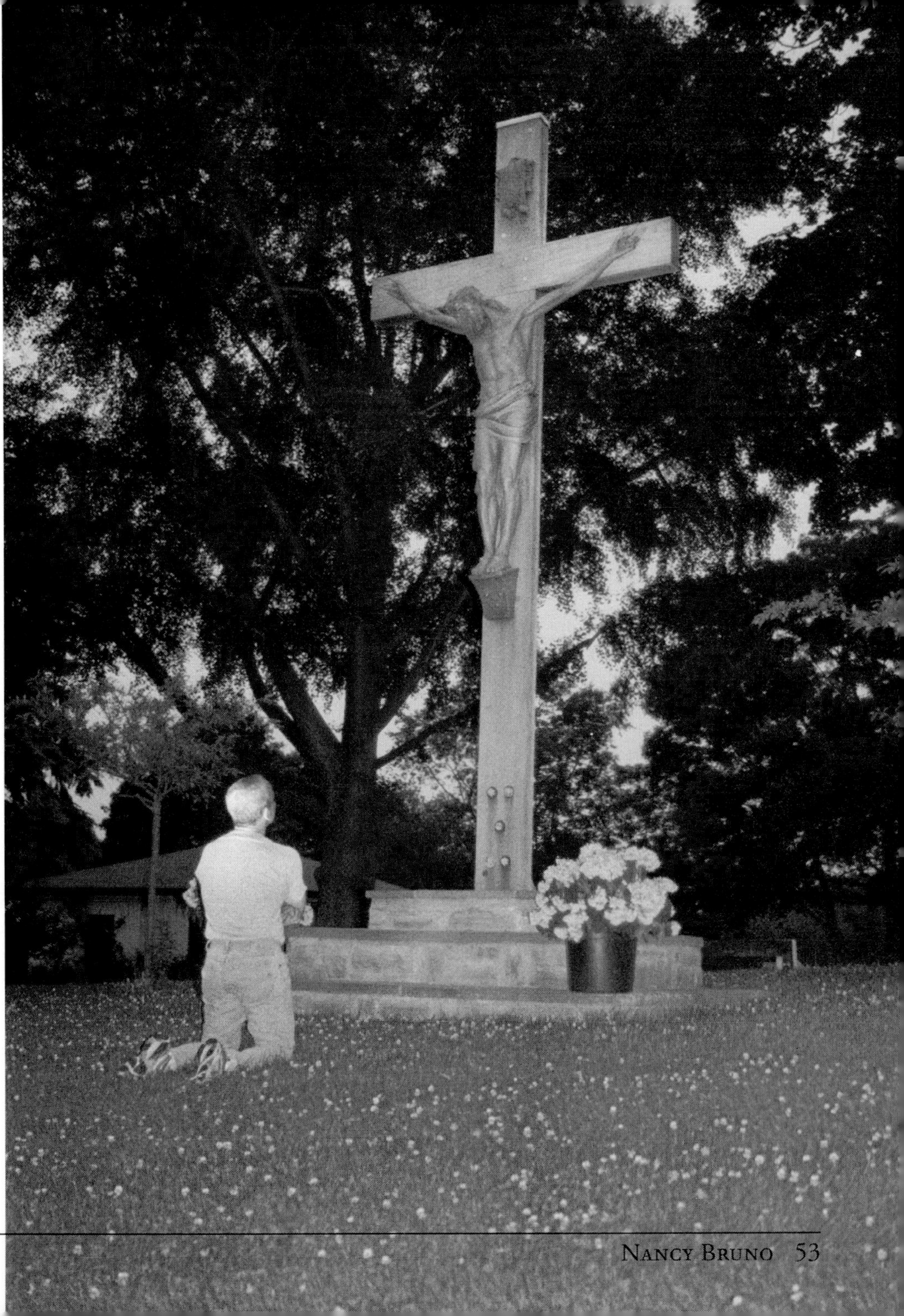

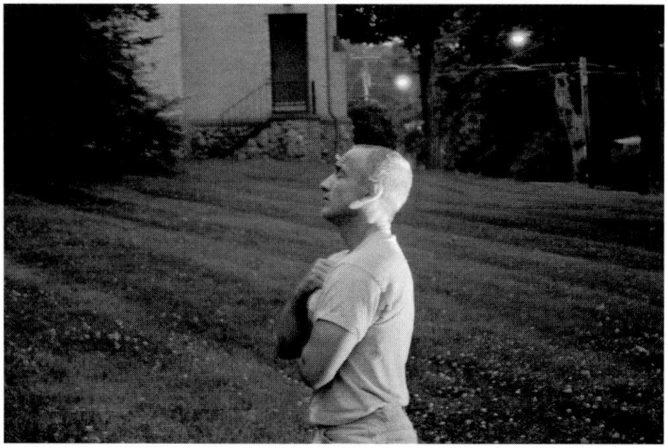

thought attracts positive events; fear and negative energy simply enables thoughts that say, “You can’t,” or, “You are not good enough,” to have a field day with your heart and soul. Fear is actually a negative prayer, and living with negative thoughts is praying for bad things to happen.

On his forty-eighth birthday Jimmy was done living in fear, living in a constant state of worry. The negative situations that surrounded and plagued him would not end until he reversed his thought process: events transpire from thoughts, thoughts develop out of beliefs, beliefs are rooted in Faith. The focus of Jimmy’s life has now shifted from the crucifixion of Jimmy to his own resurrection. He is living in a state of transformation, a direct result of the positive changes he has made in his life and all beginning with his thoughts. He knows that he is far from finished, but armed with faith and courage, he is excited to see what lies ahead when it finally arrives.

Humanity

Alfred's favorite foods are peanut butter, whipped cream, and whatever his wife makes for him. He is passionate about nature and finds meaning in a wind's whisper and peace in the stillness of the mountain air. If you passed him on the street, it would be hard to guess that he used to ride a motorcycle and owns long rifles. Alfred smiles when he is happy and perspires when he is nervous, laughs at silly stories and cries when his heart hurts. He is a man filled with strong beliefs, but out of respect for differing opinions, he is very careful not to push them onto others. Driven by not being good enough, Alfred judges himself quite harshly, yet he is incredibly fair in his evaluation of others. As a lifelong learner, Alfred is committed to personal improvement: intellectually, physically, emotionally, and spiritually. Through a great deal of reflection, he has come to understand that validation does not come from external sources, but from within. At the age of fifty, Alfred is finally comfortable in his own skin.

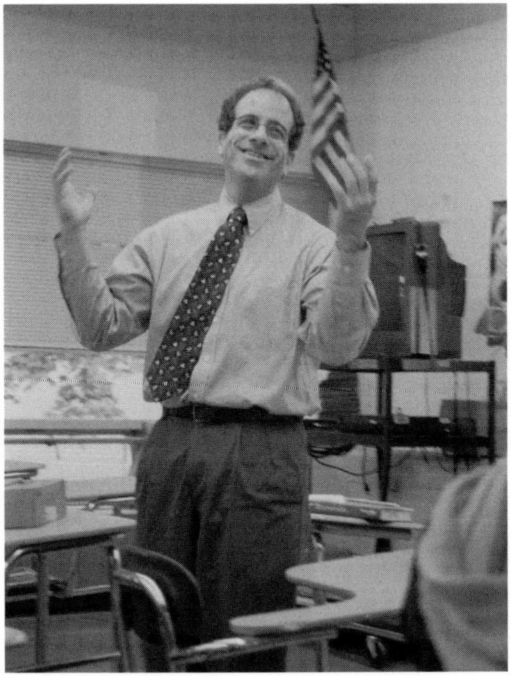

As an academic, he believes that history provides many worthwhile lessons, but he leaves himself open to all of the possibilities that the world holds. Always one to explore all of his options, Alfred is keenly aware that making a popular decision is easier than making the right decision, but then he wouldn't be able to look at himself in the mirror. Giving so much to so many, it is easy for Alfred to neglect his own interests, health, and well-being. But he knows that asking for help is not a sign of a man's weakness.

Family is the most important thing in all dimensions of Alfred's life. He is a son to his parents, the other half to his twin, brother to his siblings, husband to his wife, and father to his children. As a husband and father he has found that constant communication

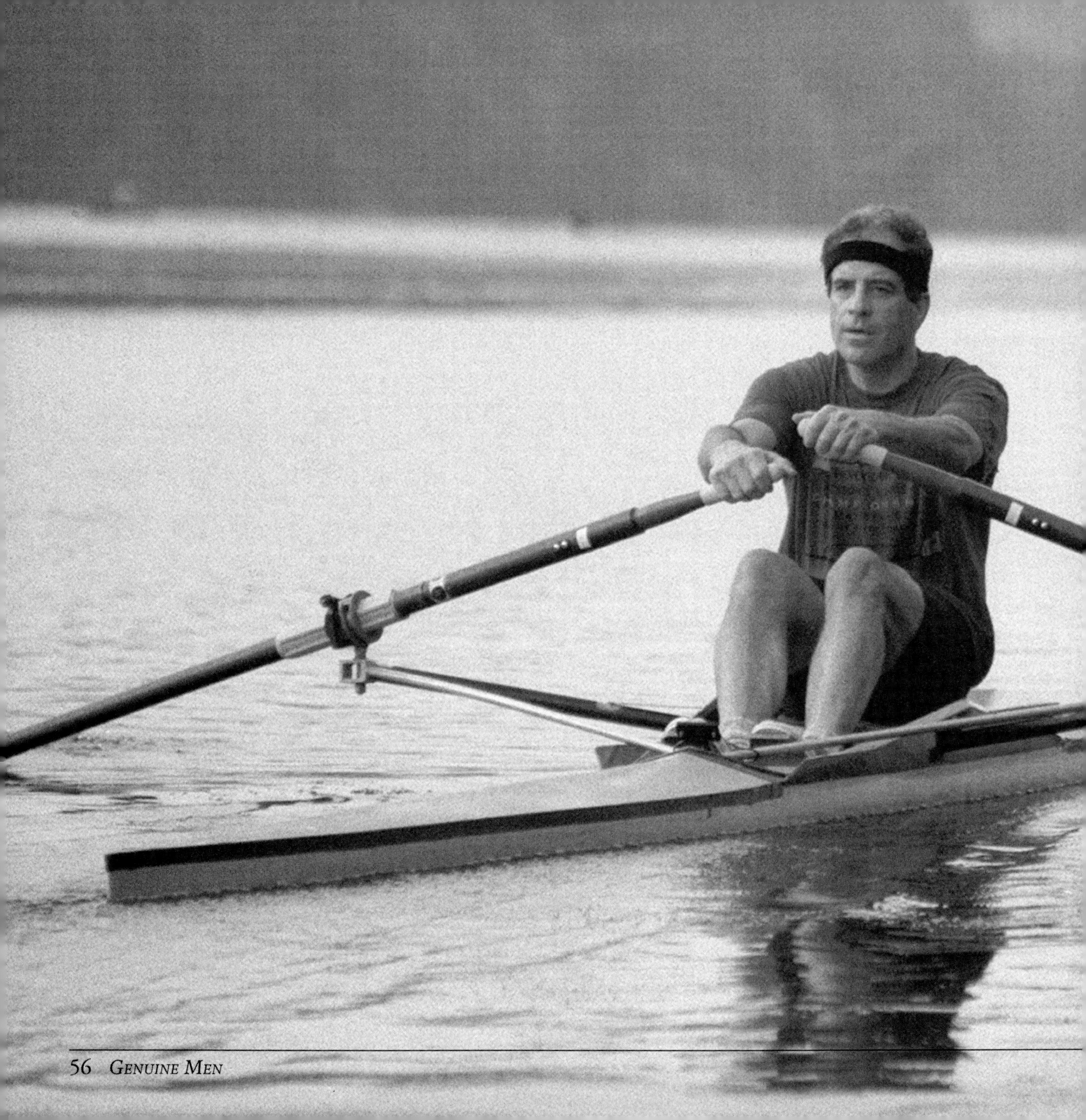

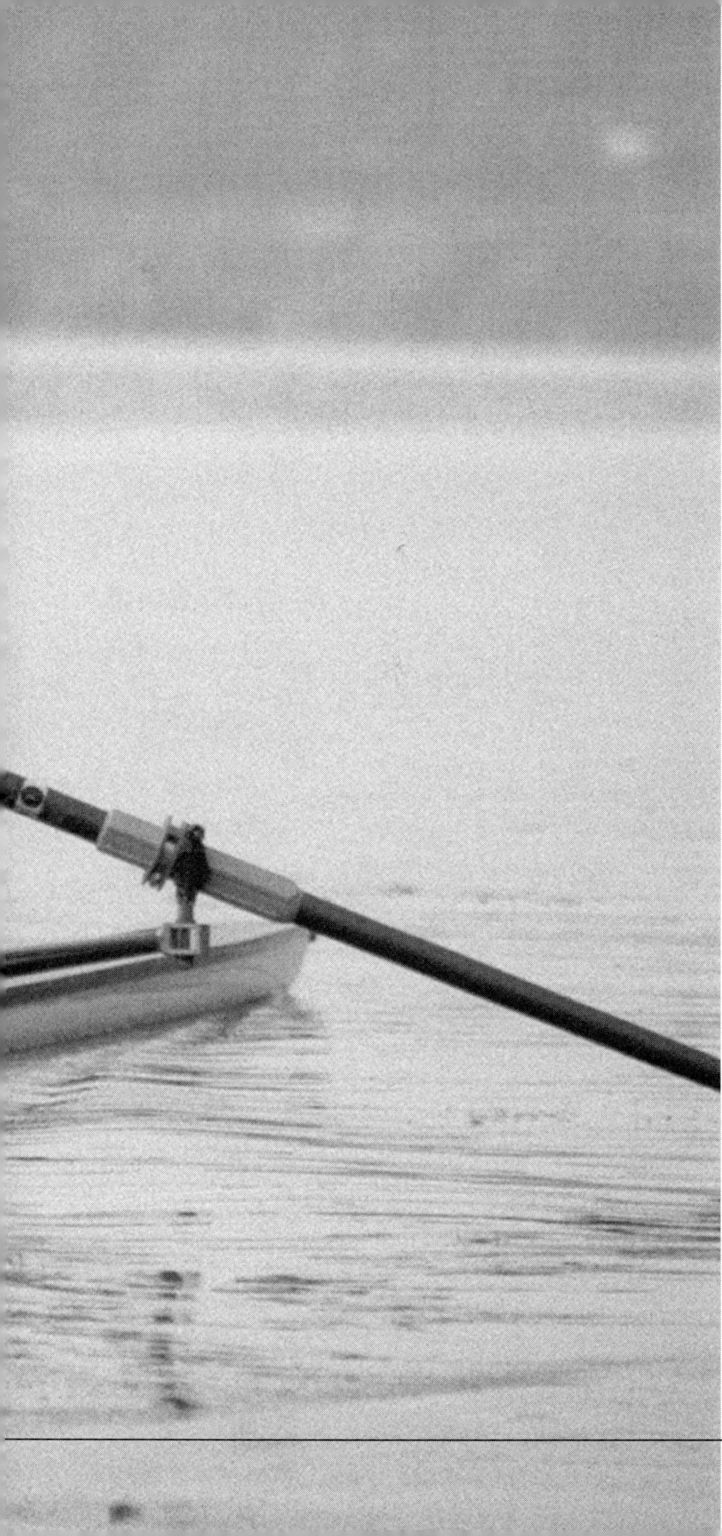

is the path to learning and growth for every member of his family. Each of his children is unique and wonderful, and he is forever learning to listen and be attentive to their needs…in a quiet way.

The greatest present is the gift of being in the moment, but his mind does drift. Is he creating lasting value? Is he making a difference? How will he pay for his daughters' college education and weddings? When will he be able to just garden, raise animals, till the land, cut trees, and live an active but simple life? This is his life, his world. This is the stuff we are all made of, this is humanity.

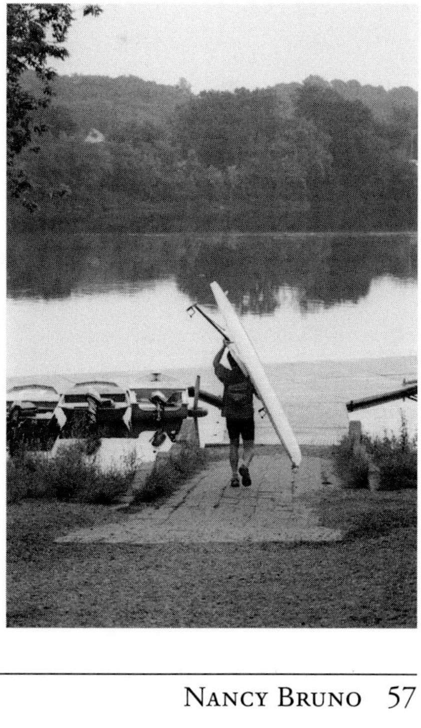

Choosing Life

He makes no excuses for his past. They are times that are behind him; he can't change his actions or decisions from days long gone. Gary is candid when he says that throughout his life he was looking for something very simple, something that everyone searches for in their lifetime: love. Unfortunately, he was looking in all of the wrong places. As a child he found fulfillment and escape in history books and encyclopedias, which took him to wonderful places and allowed his imagination to run wild. Playing and writing music allowed him to express himself, get lost, find peace. Thankfully, throughout his life, these two elements would remain havens, places he could run toward to pull him back from the brink of destruction.

As a teen, Gary was introduced to drugs. At first they were wonderful experiments in enhancing his imagination and musical experiences—it was, of course, the sixties.

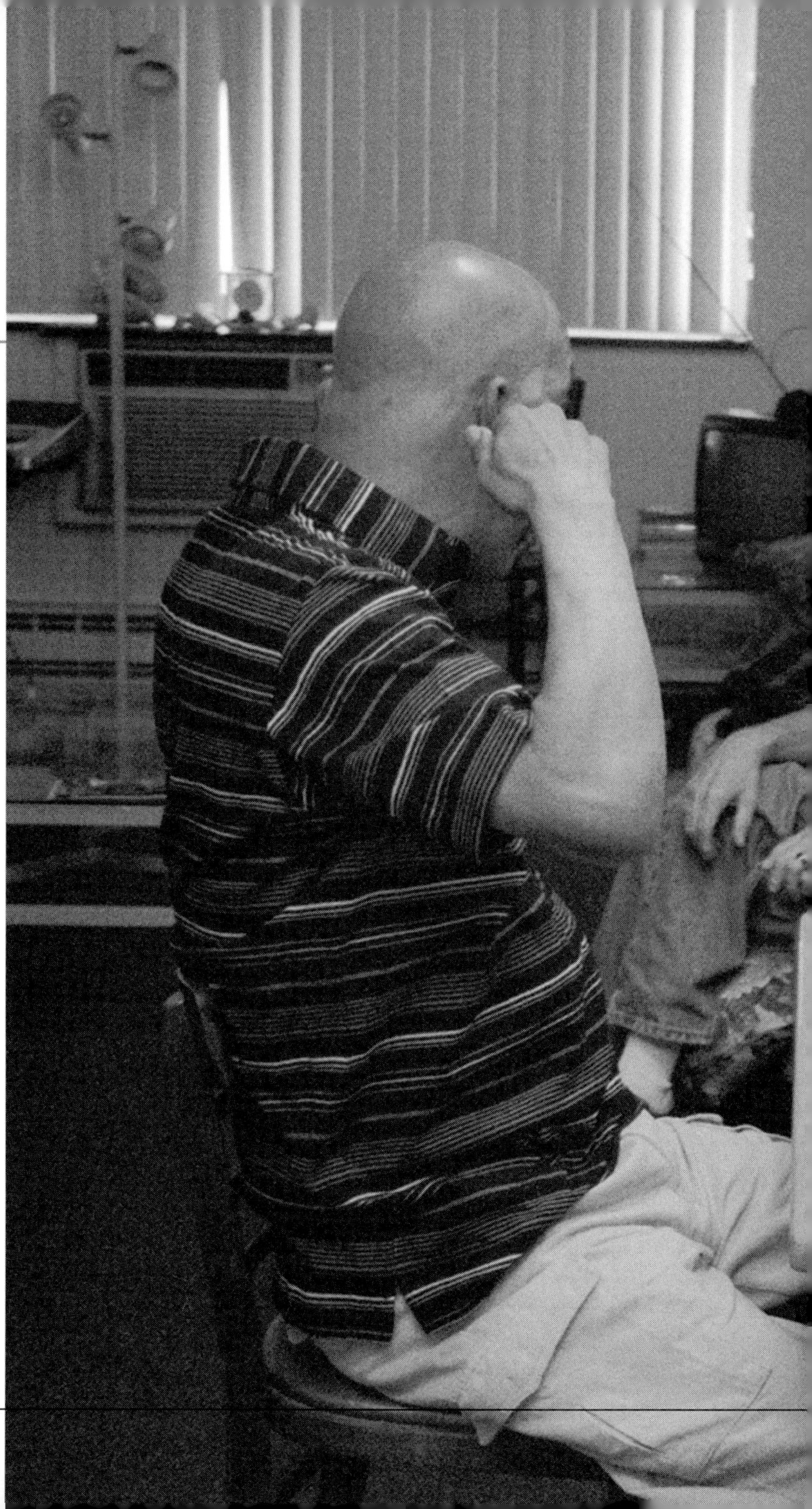

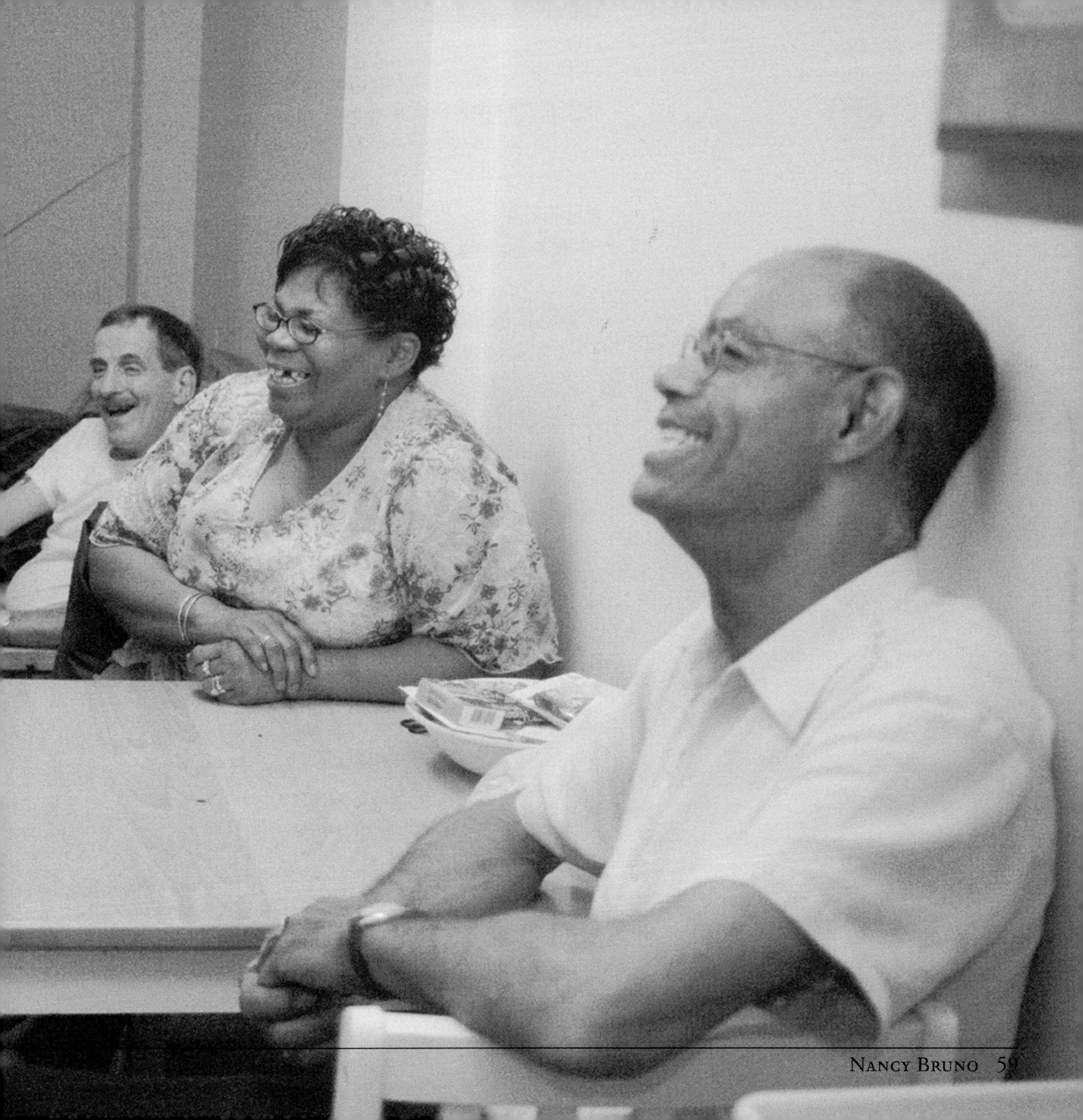

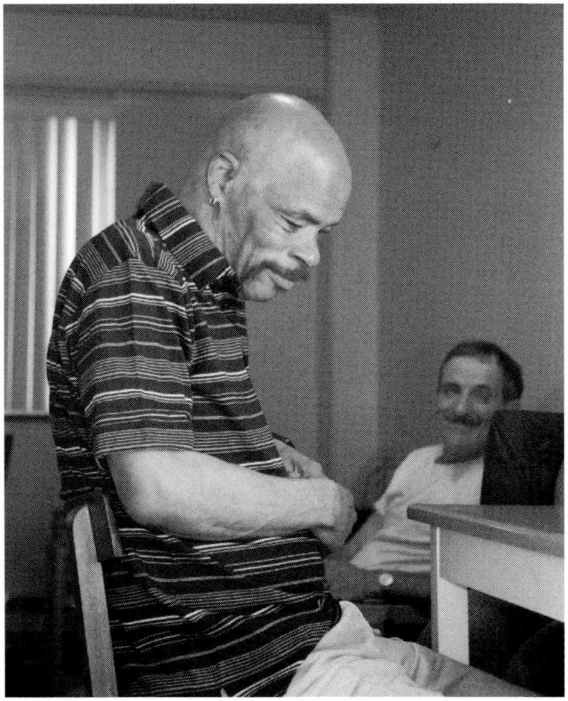

Unfortunately, innocent experimentation and a desire to be loved led Gary to embrace a lifestyle that surrounded him with people who fueled his drug habit. Thankfully, Gary was able to recognize that in his times of need and great darkness, all he needed to do was look toward the powerful blessings of his music, son, and faith in God to find his way out of temptation and imminent destruction. In a singular moment, his desire to walk away from the illusion of love led him to find a fuller meaning of love. Unfortunately, decades after relinquishing the hold that drugs had over him and living a clean and sober life, Gary was struck down with an illness that robbed him of his sight within hours and his hearing. Living in the darkness, Gary recognized that there was a simple choice to be made: be a victim of the dark silence or choose to live in the light that was life. It would be easy to place blame on others: the boys who first introduced him to drugs, his wife for leaving him with a broken heart, the doctors for misdiagnosing his illness, even God. He does not blame God. In fact, his relationship with God is peaceful and to the point. He does not blame the women from his past. In fact, he has found a woman who truly loves and accepts him for all of who he is past and present. He does not blame his family for not providing him with the kind of love and attention he needed at different points in his life. Instead, he works hard on strengthening the bonds he has with his son and brothers. No, instead of being a victim of circumstance, Gary is choosing life.

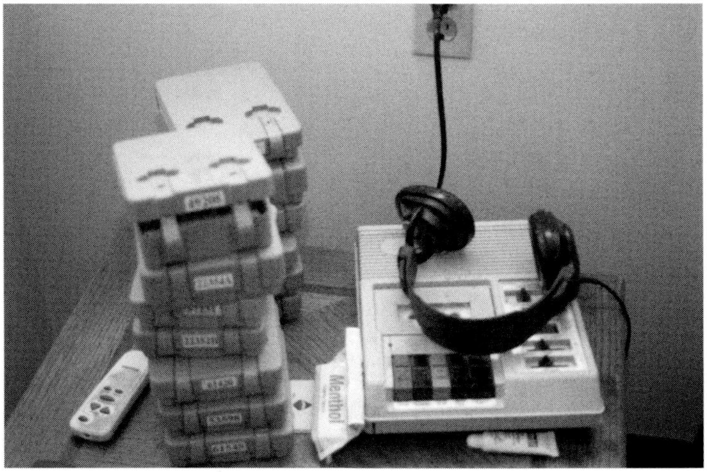

Power of Love

The power of love is transformational. It can make or break anyone, especially a man. Love can come from many different places: family, friends, personal interests, hobbies, or religion. Yet, the most important love comes from within. As a boy, Cliff was one of eighteen children and part of a family whose patriarch led with an iron fist. Cliff was a true athlete: he not only excelled at his chosen sports but earned the respect of his teammates and coaches. They became his family; they believed in him, they supported him, and ultimately, they loved him. When his father found out that he was sneaking away to play sports instead of doing his chores, he broke his arm. When Cliff was fifteen, his father passed away, and Cliff was placed in a foster family. For the first time in his life Cliff was surrounded by unconditional love. This was all that he needed to be released from the pain and hardship of his past and begin living. Cliff met a young girl who he would love like no other, and they wed after high school. Then, in an instant, his marriage came crashing down around him, the love was gone, and Cliff was a broken man—emotionally, physically, and spiritually.

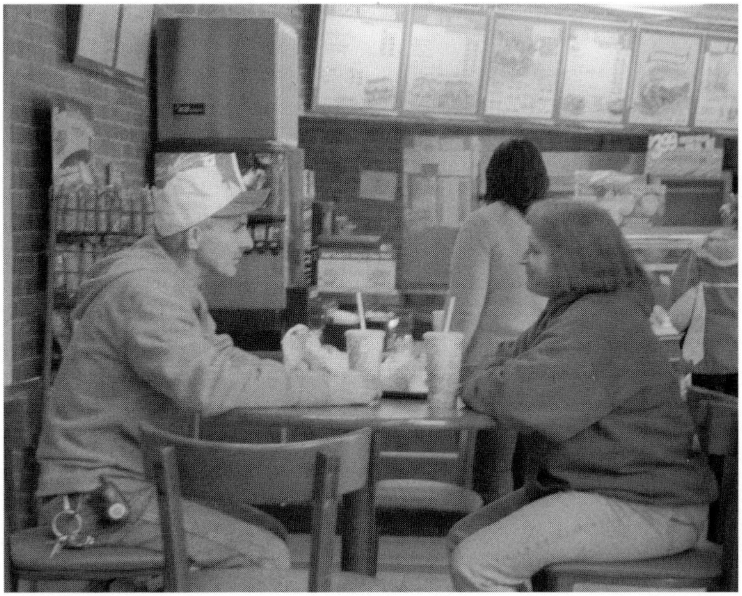

For the next twenty years, Cliff clung to the pain of his past, punishing himself night after night with the belief that he was a bad person. Despite remarrying a woman who loved him and beginning a family of his own, their love and support couldn't change the way he felt about himself. Any change that was going to happen needed to begin within Cliff. As the lives of those he loved most continued to move forward, Cliff's life was going nowhere because

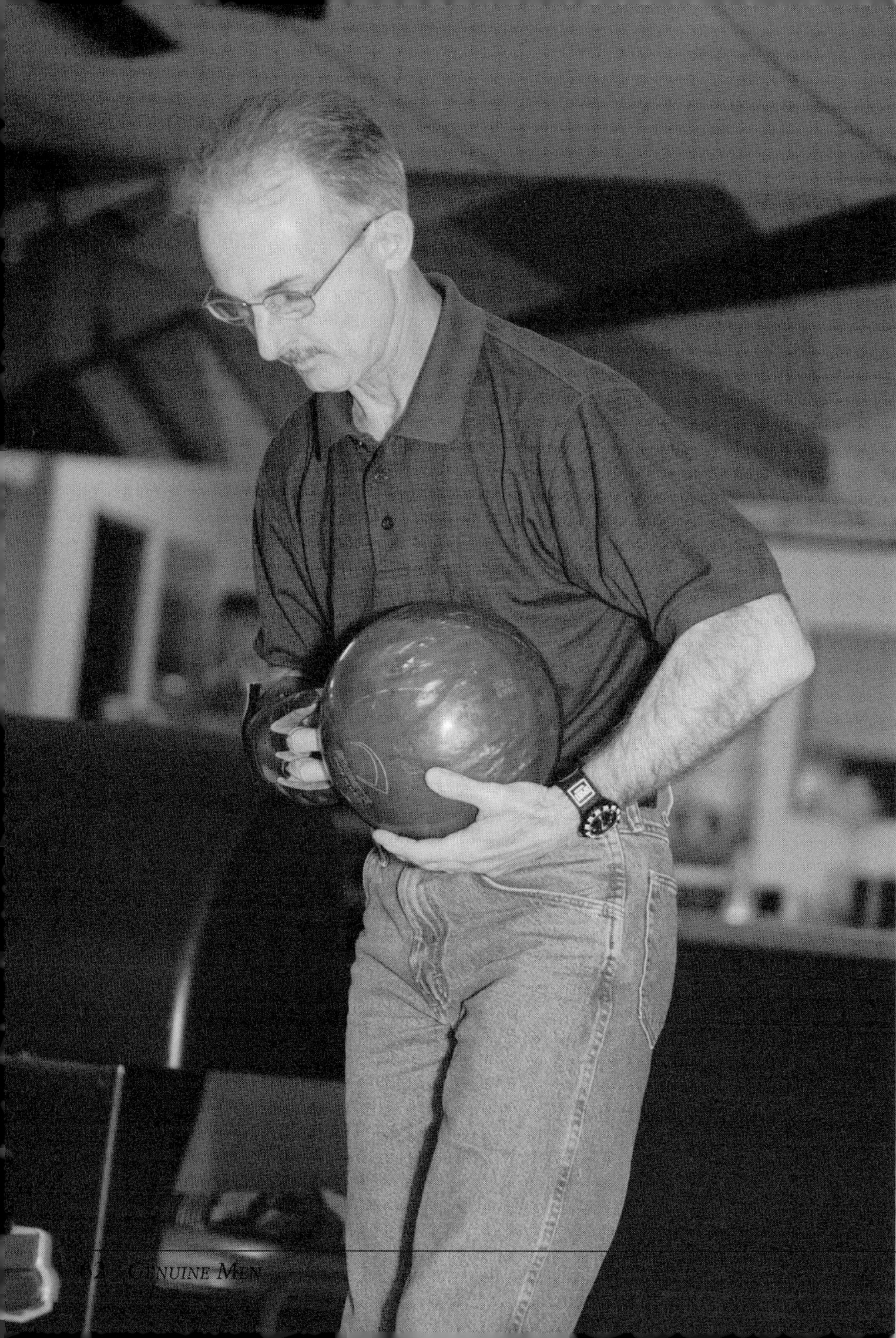

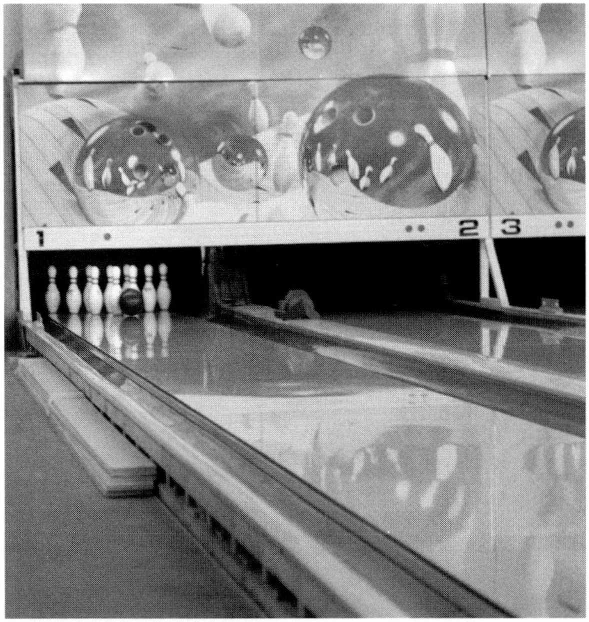

he chose alcohol over everything else life had to offer. He lost jobs, he lost friends, he lost chances of happiness for himself and his family, and in seeing all of this he lost respect for himself. It was time to let go of the pain of the past and move forward, time to see and love himself as those who knew him best saw and loved him. It was time to put down the bottle. In that moment of recognition Cliff stood up and declared to those he loved what they already knew, and had waited so many years for him to acknowledge: “That’s it, I’m done. I have a problem. I need my life back. I need to change. I need help.”

Ten years later, Cliff works on his sobriety every single day. He cherishes his present and looks forward to the future with hope. He has transformed himself into the type of man that he knew he could always be: a good father and grandfather, a good employee, a good friend, a good coach, and a respected part of his community. Perhaps what he is most proud of is that he is now someone who others turn to for help and advice in their times of trouble. When Cliff is asked how he was able to turn his life around he immediately responds by saying that none of it would have been possible without the patience and unwavering love of his wife, Robin. She was the light at the end of his dark journey, standing and waiting for him to make it to the other side. She understood that Cliff needed to do this in his own time, and in his own way; she could only love him through to the end.

The Truth Lives Within

As a teen, Bob bought what would be the first of many guitars, learning basic chords from a nun on public television. The experience created a spark deep within, bright enough to get him through dark moments, but not yet strong enough to fuel a brewing passion. During high school he worked as a printer's apprentice, helping to get the village newspaper out so there were things to talk about around town. It was interesting enough, and important to the people who read the paper, but it was just a way to make some extra money. Playing with his band on the weekends was a different story. The money wasn't great, but there was nothing like the roar of an audience at the end of a set. The spark fully ignited, Bob gave in to his life's passion. He dove headfirst with his eyes closed into songwriting, figuring that it was just about playing whatever gigs came his way.

After a while, the dream of a musician's life gave way to the reality of living in a tiny apartment with no money to spend after paying the rent. Self-doubt began to creep in. Maybe he just wasn't supposed to be a musician; music would have to take a backseat for a while. A job fell into his lap, and in time it turned out that he was pretty good at it.

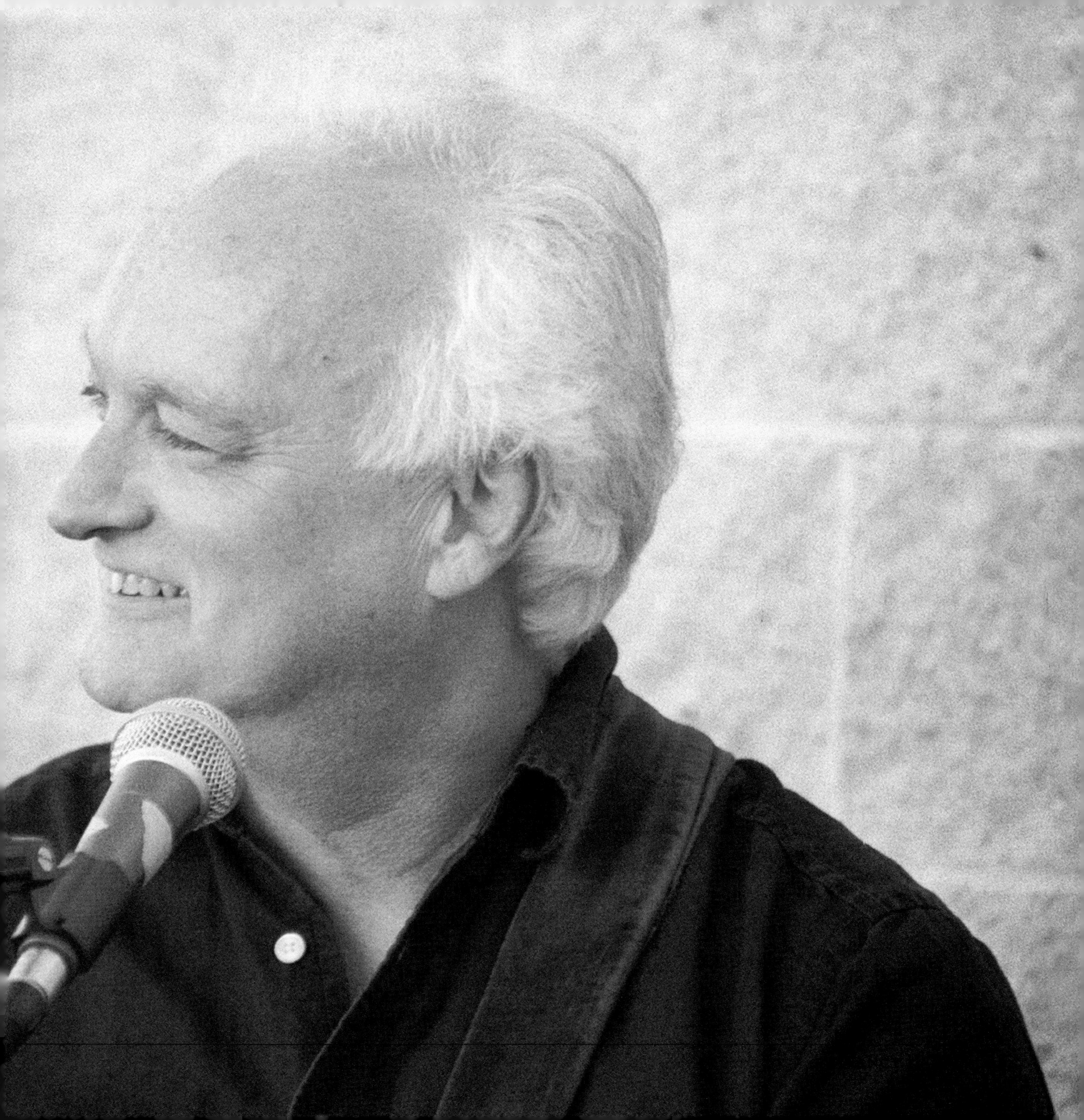

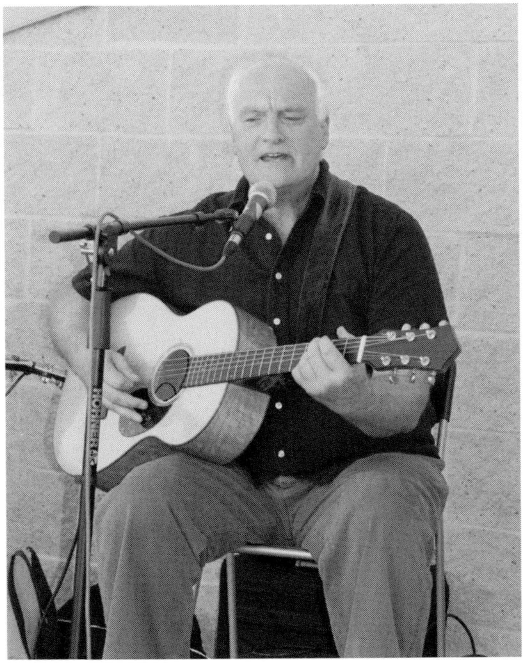

The pay was steady, he had extra cash to spend as he pleased, and eventually he was in a position to provide a comfortable life for his family. Yet, as the years passed Bob never stopped feeling like a songwriter, and despite his reverence for honesty, he wasn't being honest with himself. Yes, he was a forty-nine-year-old man with responsibilities to his family that included a mortgage, bills, and his son's college education, but somehow he knew there are some truths too important to deny.

In the moment he chose to no longer do something that he did not love, to be someone he no longer wanted to be; he chose to make everything else happen. Bob knew that in order to succeed, this time had to be different; he had to be different. This was not going to be the same free-spirited youthful adventure of years gone by but a thought-out and planned journey. There would have to be sacrifices: times he would have to teach instead of attending one of his son's baseball games, weekends performing out of town when he would rather be home with his family. He was in for the long haul. It hasn't been easy, but it has made him a stronger writer, a better performer, and a well-respected husband and father. Bob's always considered himself to be a late bloomer, and he is quite happy just where he is in the moment. Since he began living his truth, his life certainly hasn't gotten any easier, but it does get better every day.

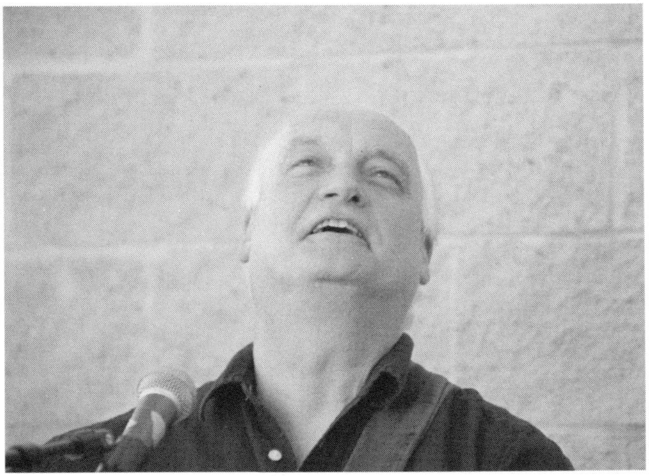

To Be a Man

Growing up, Juan believed that there was no greater accomplishment than to be a man. From where he stood, the men had it all: respect, power, and the most meat on their plate. Juan, like all little boys, was completely unaware of the challenges, sacrifices, and responsibilities that came with being a man. At the time of his youth, the Dominican Republic was a country embroiled in civil turmoil. Juan grew up in the capital city of Santo Domingo, where there were frequent military and civil confrontations. There was also a great deal of excitement for a boy living amid all of the action. With Juan's father at sea for stretches at a time, Juan and his brother were reared by a multi-generational collective of women: his mother, grandmother, and teachers.

A day came when Juan's parents knew that it was in the best interest of their family to leave their homeland. Juan clearly remembers walking to the Dominican Naval Headquarters, standing before a panel of powerful-looking military men, and watching his mother give unwavering testimony and answering questions on behalf of her family's visa application. Somewhat taken aback by the brute appearance of these men, Juan almost did not see the man listening intently to his mother at the end of the table. The truth was that these men looked powerful but held no authority—that belonged to the unassuming American attaché at the end of the table. With a quiet nod of this gentleman's head, Juan and his family were granted an opportunity for a new life. Juan's family moved to New York City where he learned English, attended school, and began to understand his new culture. He was aware of what his parents gave up and left behind, and he was not going to let them down.

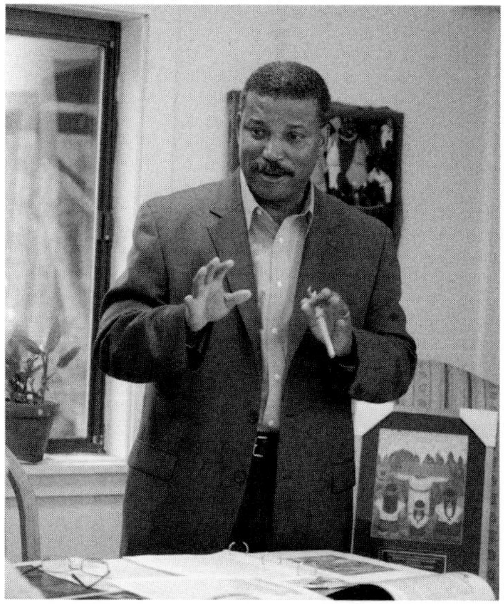

Juan learned many things during his four years in college, but as one might suspect, the most important life lesson was not taught to him within the four walls of a classroom. In order to be the kind of

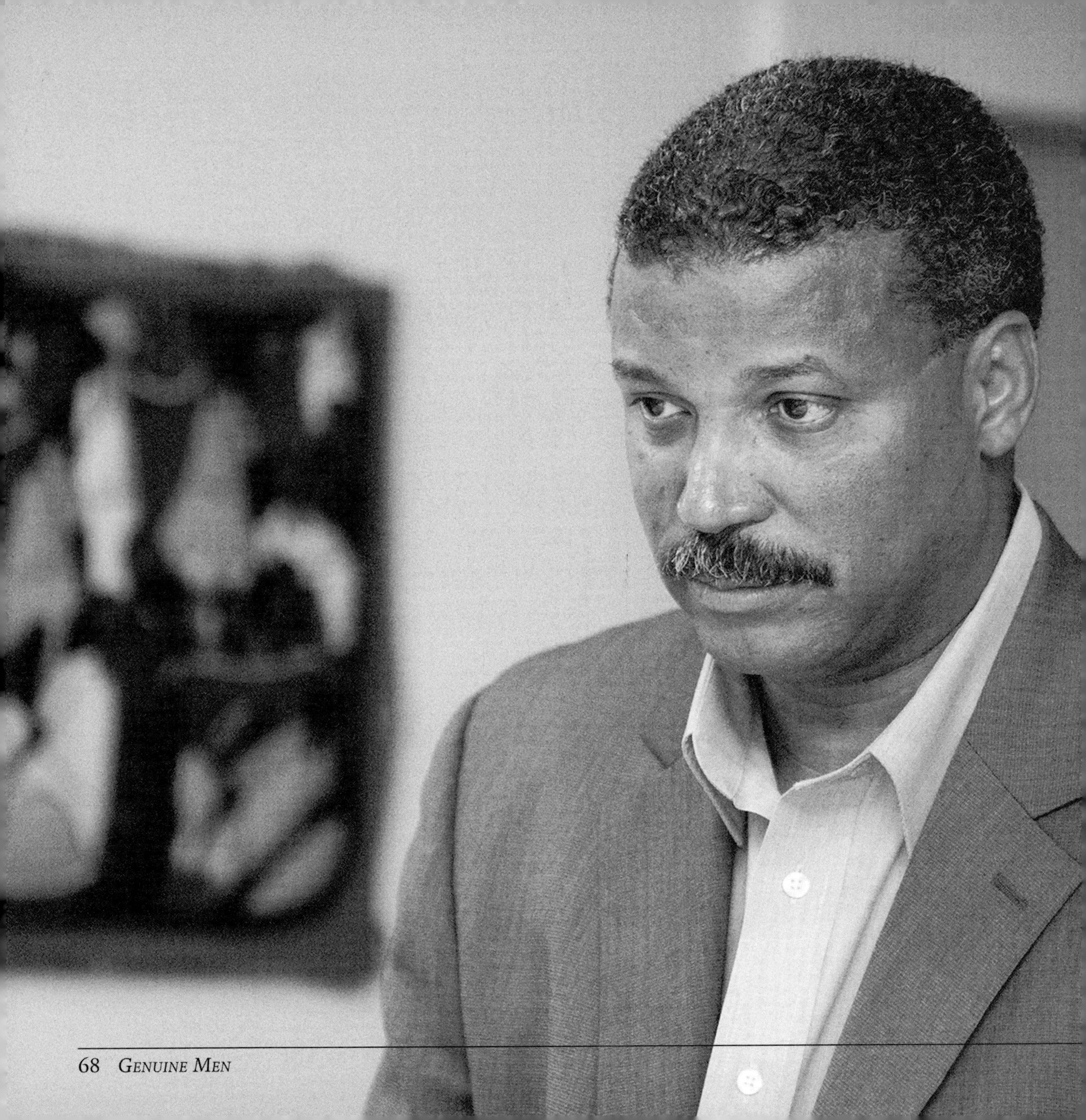

man he wanted to be in life, Juan needed to acknowledge that he was weighed down with a great deal of baggage. The time had come for him to unpack the articles from the past that were not his to carry forward and choose the pieces of himself to hold on to and cultivate. It was an exercise in self-awareness, and Juan was able to look upon his life and know that every experience and encounter shaped the man whose reflection he saw in the mirror.

Now, he is a respected businessman and civic leader, a beloved grandfather, and a catalyst for positive change in his community. All of this is possible because he continues to pay attention to what is shaping him, unpack and repack his baggage, and grow and change. He embraces the challenges, sacrifices, and responsibilities that come with being a man, an honor that he does not take for granted.

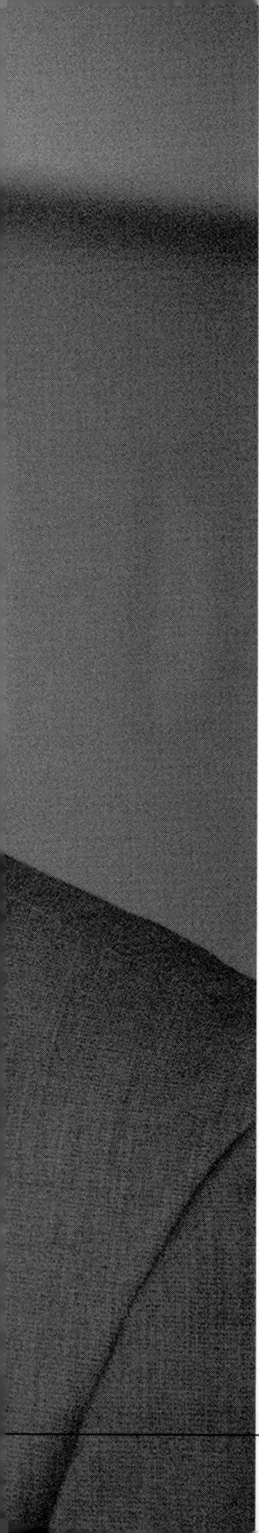

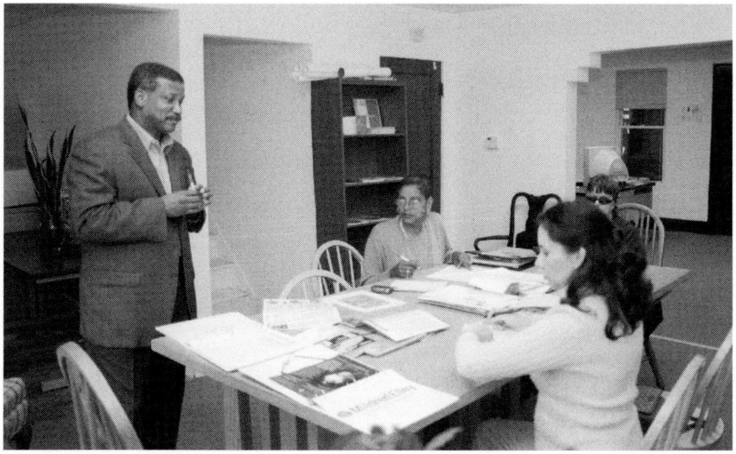

Making the Most of Life's Challenges

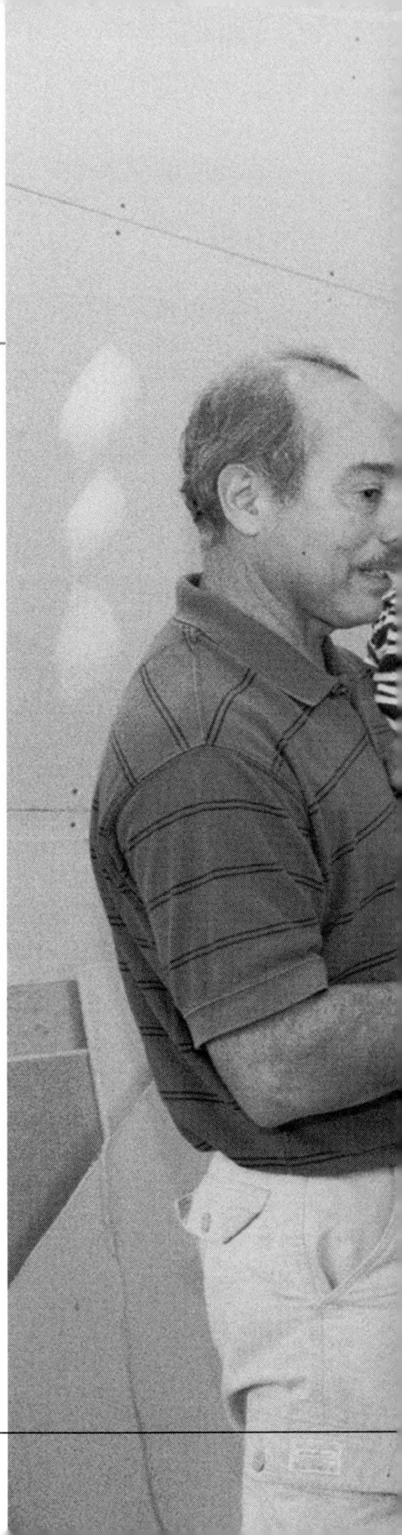

Ramon's approach to life has enabled him to overcome many challenges, the first being the loss of his parents as a young child. After years of living with surrogate families, at the age of fourteen, Ramon began envisioning a better life for himself. He went to live at an orphanage run by the Brothers of the Holy Cross. The Brothers were much more than caretakers; they were mentors, father figures, educators, and leaders.

The boys who displayed discipline and the potential to succeed outside the orphanage attended public school. This privilege opened up a new world for Ramon, encouraging him to develop friendships, participate on public school sports teams, and foster relationships with families. Ramon was able to observe these families modeling the core values he wanted to one day pass on to his children: hard work, honesty, discipline, balance, contribution, and community. At seventeen, with high school graduation approaching, Ramon knew that education represented the door to opportunity, and he wanted to go to college. He continued on to a four-year school, and one of the proudest moments of his life is the day he graduated college. Ramon was filled with a tremendous amount of joy for his accomplishments, was excited for what lay ahead, and was daunted by the notion of facing a world full of opportunity alone.

The safety net was gone. Once again, he needed to dig down and find what he was made of. He took stock of what he did have: an inner strength that enabled him to be positive, a deep sense of self, a set of core values, a work ethic,

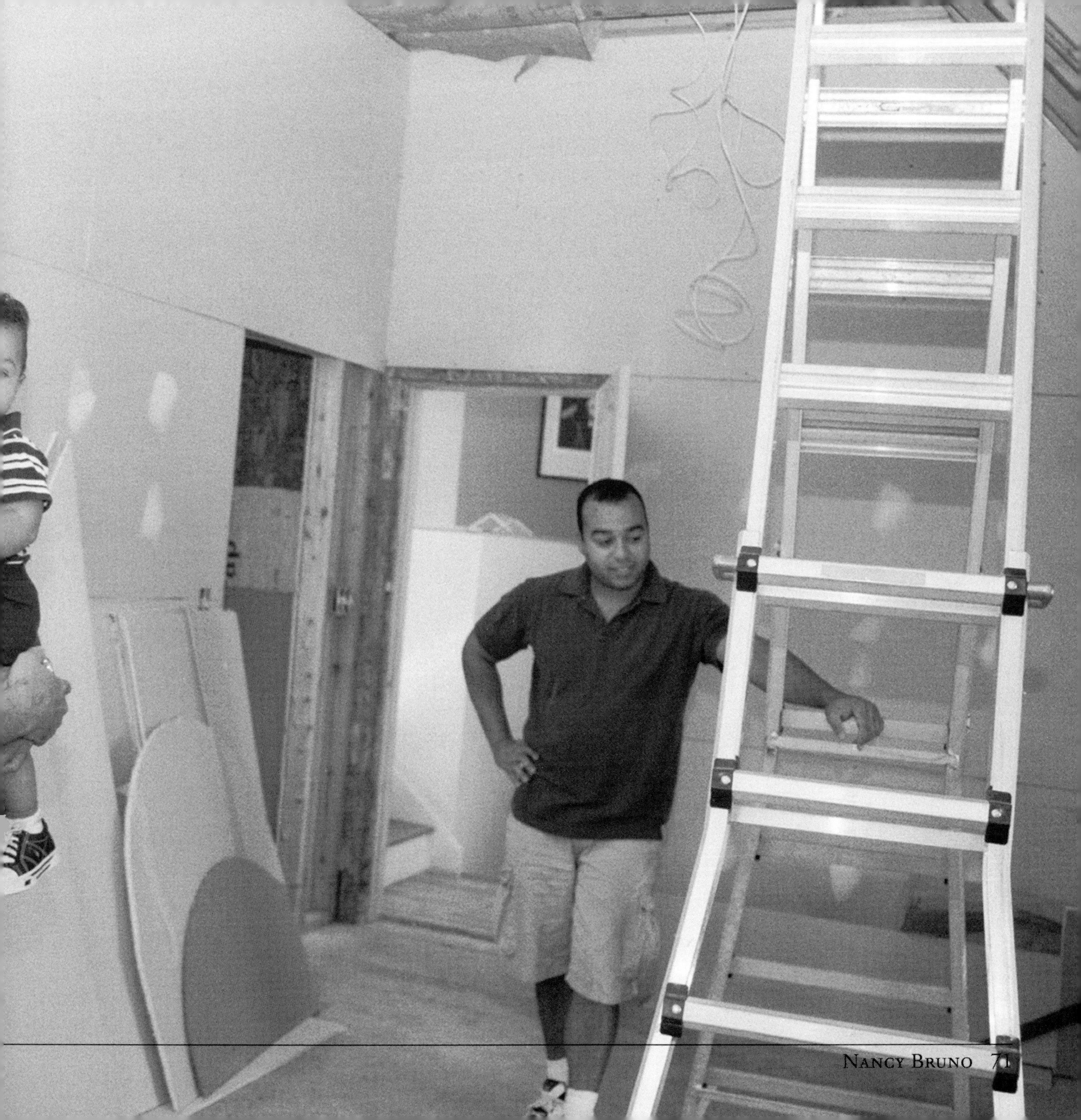

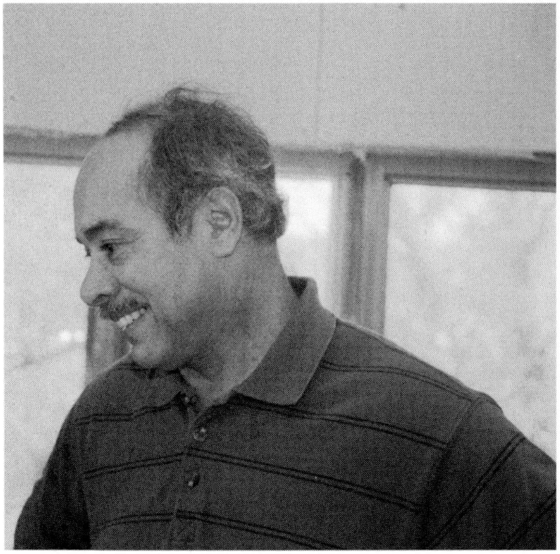

and an education that held the promise of great opportunities. His internal compass in place, he set out to thrive, not simply survive. As a husband and father he created a successful family with a woman he calls his wife, partner, friend, and confidante. He believes that family is one's legacy and that providing children with the tools to build their own compass is the purpose of parenting.

Now, as a grandfather, Ramon is looking forward to taking on a completely new role: helping his young grandchildren uncover their gifts, develop their character, and explore the traits and abilities that will enable them to thrive. He values friendship and being a member of the community, helping and sharing with others in good times and bad. He approaches his colleagues with respect and honors their contributions, holding them to the same high expectations he has for himself. To an outsider looking in, one would not know Ramon emerged from such meager beginnings. His ability to view the world through the positive lenses of possibility has enabled him to overcome life's challenges and make positive contributions to society. A great deal of the credit goes to the Brothers of the Holy Cross. They taught him not to be shaped by trauma, but to take control of his life by being prepared for opportunities and making choices. The rest he graciously accepts as a blessing and a gift.

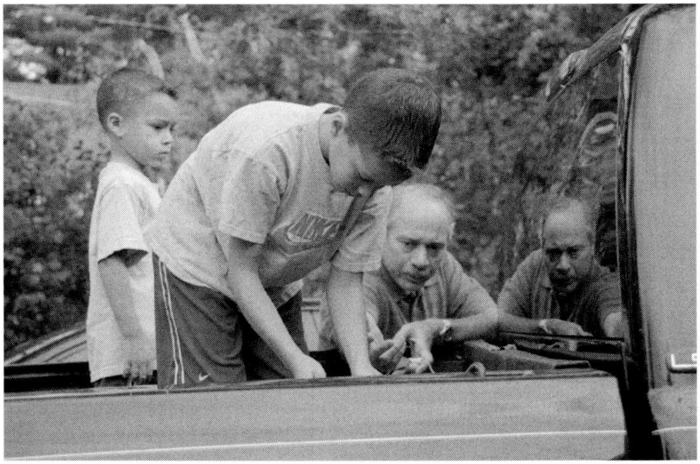

Building for Success

Bruce's life has been filled with diverse experiences. He has grown from the challenging ones, has been gratified by the fulfilling ones, and has been humbled by the breadth of opportunities that he has enjoyed over the years. Early in life, Bruce learned that in order to be successful he needed to rely on his ability to bring together, and motivate, people as a team. His father, possessing an entrepreneurial spirit, chose to leave the comfort of a full-time job and purchased a farm. At the age of thirteen, Bruce was put in charge of his family's tobacco farm. From the time he was a kid in middle school, he was the person responsible for hiring workers, watching over the crops, and managing the team of workers he relied upon to take care of the day-to-day running of the tobacco farm.

Despite his many responsibilities on the farm, Bruce did find time to enjoy just being a kid. He stood only five feet, eight inches, but he was a good shot on the court. On and off the court, Bruce's teammates looked to him for motivation and leadership. When Bruce went off to college, he decided to join a fraternity. While living in a house with other brothers he learned to contend with different personalities, trust his instincts, and from weekly poker games, to read faces.

His mother was a vivacious young woman who passed on to her son her heart, values, and work ethic; these gifts have turned out to be some of Bruce's greatest assets. Bruce was just a few years out of college, and his wife was expecting their first child, when a drunk driver killed his mother. Bruce only wishes that his mother had the opportunity to know her grandchildren.

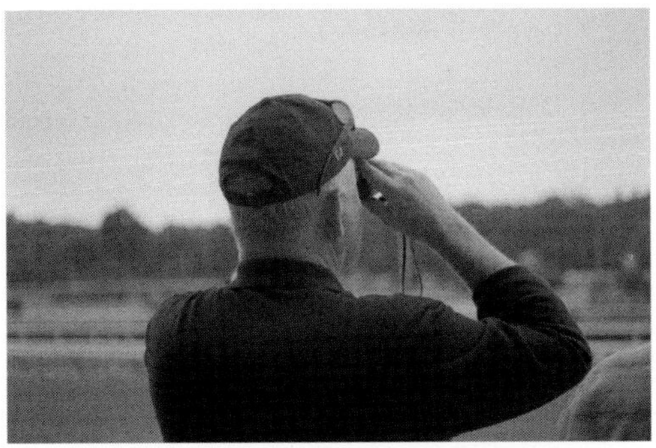

Raising three daughters was completely uncharted territory for Bruce, and he was working without a map or a compass. His children looked to him for leadership, guidance, motivation, discipline, support, and love. Parental instinct served him well, and he knew that in order to make these girls successful, he needed

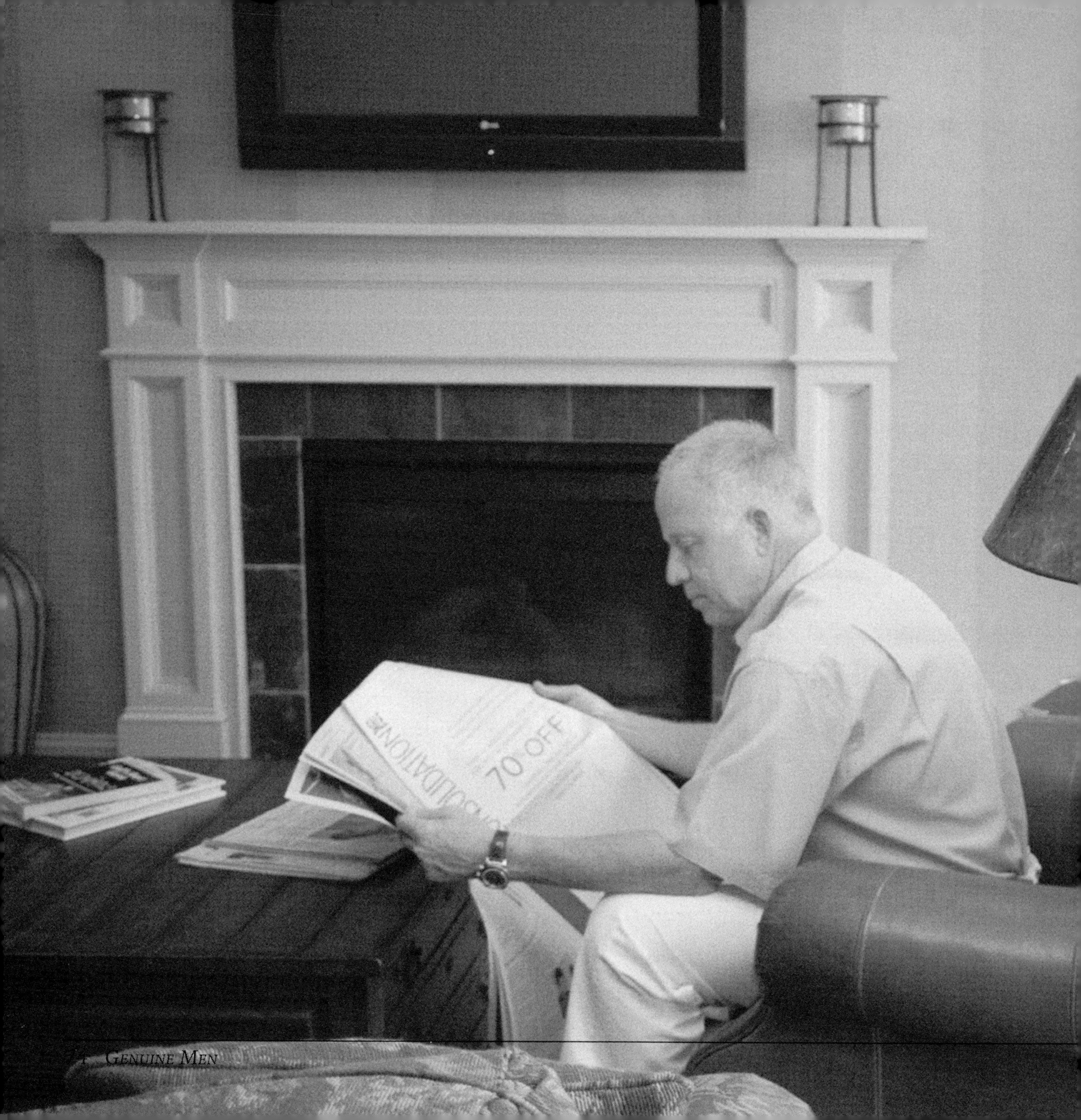
70 OFF

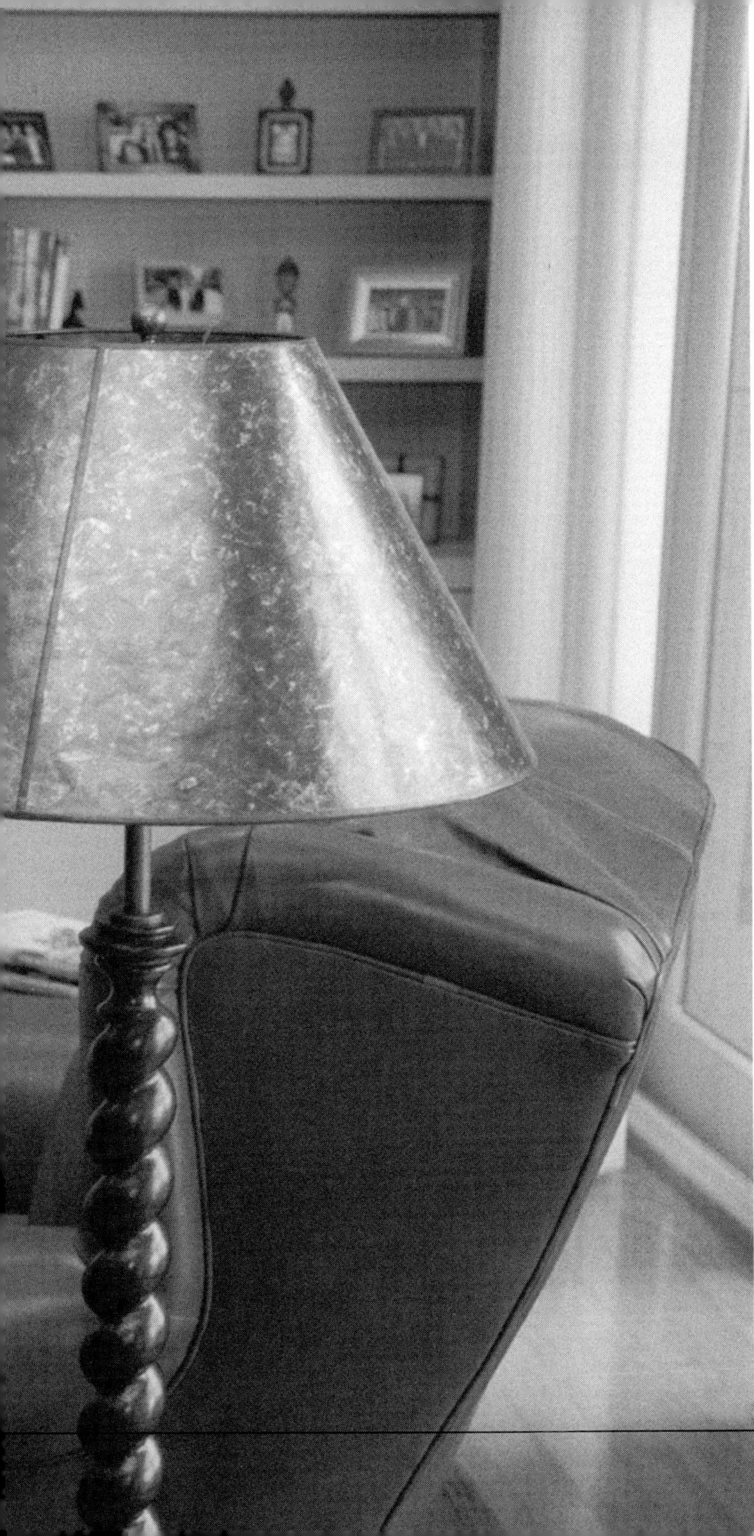

to assume many different roles as a parent. Unlike in his professional life, he could not delegate: he had to be everything to everyone, even if it did wear him down. At some of his lowest points he would take a moment and think about the people who inspired him throughout his life—his fantasy dream team—and what they did to overcome their challenges. One in particular, W.T. Young, shared with Bruce what he did when faced with a complex problem: simplify it, accept it, or just work around it. Bruce has applied Young's sage advice in business, politics, horses, and family. Regardless of whether the venture is professional or personal, Bruce always strives for success and longevity; in his mind the concepts are not mutually exclusive. The team-building process begins with Bruce looking inward and taking stock of what he brings to the table. He is objective about his strengths and painfully aware of his weaknesses. He knows that there is no room for arrogance, especially his own.

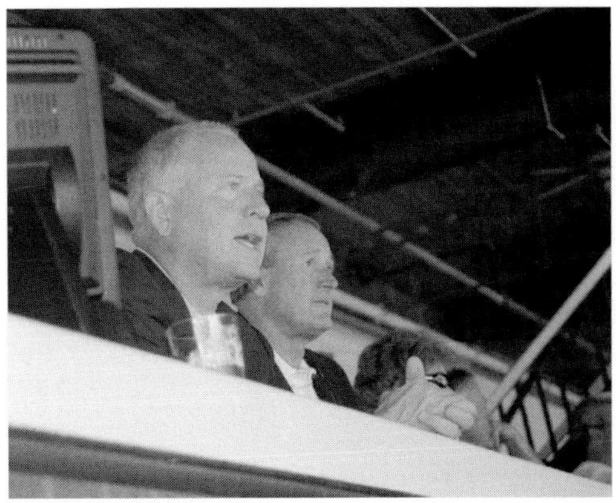

Determination + Hard Work
Success

Hugh is a man of quiet determination, always combining his natural abilities and hard work to achieve his goals. As a boy Hugh loved horses, and when he turned twelve he was given a yearling colt that he named Rebel. His parents knew nothing about horses, but they knew their son and placed the responsibility upon him for the care and training of the much-desired gift. He spent hours working with his horse, applying knowledge from books, from talking with horsemen, and from his own sense of what was right for his horse. It all came together, and a year later Hugh and Rebel were galloping across farms and open fields.

Hugh's interest in competitive sports began in high school, where he competed in tennis, swimming, and cross country running. Hugh excelled at running, but there was something special about being in the water. His college swim coach noted that although Hugh was not the team's star swimmer, he gave each race everything he had, and that made him tough to beat.

When Hugh finished college he was twenty years old and really didn't know what he wanted to do in life. After being drawn to the Navy, he was selected for and then graduated from Naval Officer Candidate School. It was the Vietnam era, and this young man found the unknown very exciting. This newly commissioned ensign put in for assignment to BUDS, Basic Underwater Demolition SEAL training. It was with focus and determination that he persevered through what was reputed to be the toughest six-month course of military training, followed by additional training to jump out of airplanes, lock out of submarines, and deliver a nuclear weapon. He ultimately was assigned to SEAL Team Two and command of the Second Platoon. In August of 1962 he and his men were on their way to Vietnam. Early on, a combat wound resulted in the amputation of his right index

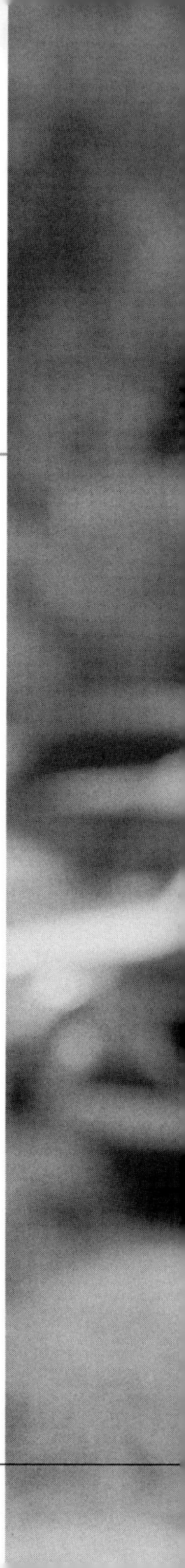

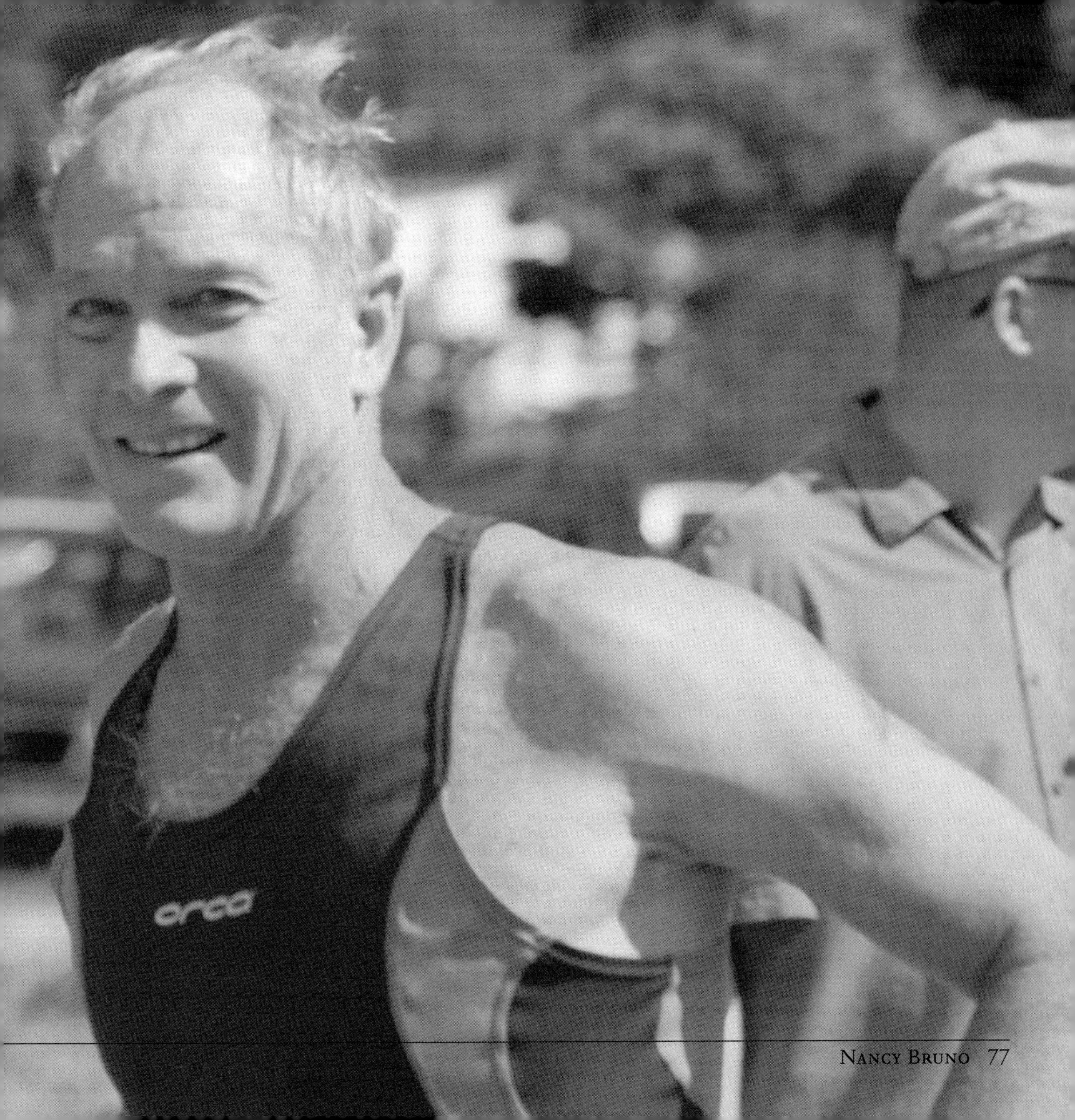
orca

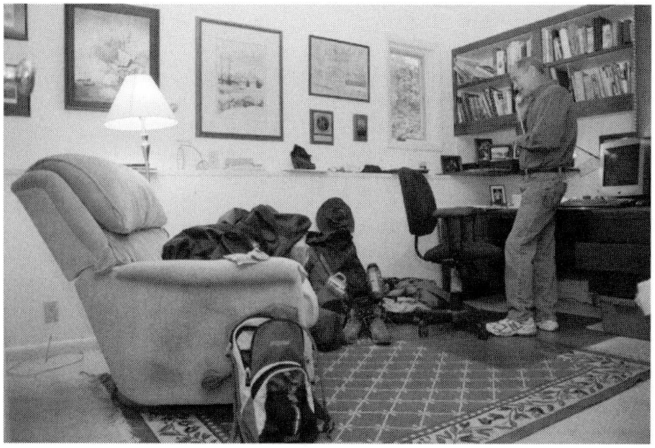

finger. It was his ticket home, but after breaking in a new trigger finger, he resumed command. Eventually, the stress of combat operations and making life-and-death decisions began to take its toll on this young green officer. Hugh's angst and concern became visible to a senior petty officer, who pulled him aside. "Sir, you do everything you can, and after that there's no point in worrying." These few words served Hugh long after leaving the jungles and the rice paddies of Vietnam.

When Hugh became a father, he accepted the responsibilities of parenthood as he had accepted those of the yearling colt and his platoon. He did all he could do to provide for his daughter's physical and emotional needs, directing and leading her on the path to a happy and healthy life. Always the athlete himself, Hugh competes in triathlons all over the country. Practicing what he preaches, he trains hard to achieve the goals he sets for himself, focusing on *his* swim, *his* run, and *his* cycling times. Don't be mistaken, Hugh loves competing, especially with men in younger age categories. Come race days he knows that he has trained his body and it will perform to the best of its ability.

His body has always served him well as a swimmer, a Navy SEAL, and an elite athlete, but twelve years ago he was diagnosed with prostate cancer. Cancer has been his life's greatest challenge, and he faces it with the quiet determination of a SEAL, doing what is necessary to overcome the disease. Until the day his doctors tell him that he is in remission, he cohabitates with his cancer, choosing to die with it instead of worrying about dying because of it.

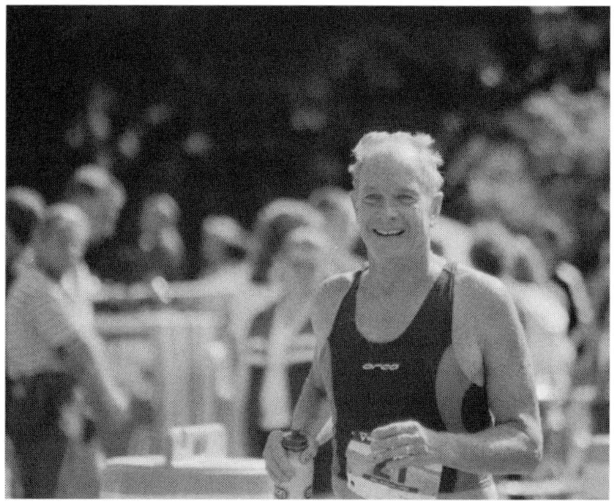

Hugh begins each morning with the same ritual he has had since his navy days, doing a set of push-ups. It is becoming increasingly more difficult to complete the set, but it is not the cancer that makes sixty-three push-ups a challenge. As his arms begin to tire, he refocuses, and with quiet determination he digs in to achieve his goal.

Doing What You Love, Loving What You Do

As a little boy, Joe didn't want to be a firefighter, baseball player, or an astronaut. When he grew up, Joe wanted to be a radio broadcaster. From the radio speakers he heard more than just rhythm and melodies; he heard humanity in the voices of the men speaking to his family. Joe was inspired by these radiomen: Herb Oscar Anderson, the best and most respected morning DJ on the East Coast, and Dan Ingram, an afternoon drive-time personality—both voices heard over the airwaves of the most popular station in North America; Dave Maynard, a midday DJ whom Joe listened to on summer days when he was not in school; and Dick Biondi, a true master of creating a radio show that touched the human spirit.

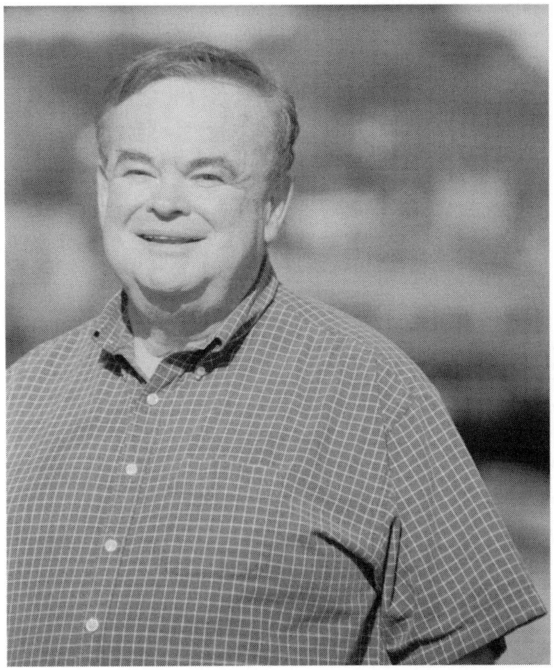

At the age of sixteen, Joe had his first radio show. It wasn't from his basement or an extracurricular activity at school; Joe had his own Sunday night radio show for a local radio station. It was the rock 'n' roll era, and as a disc jockey he wanted to spin the contemporary versions of the songs he listened to with his parents and grandparents growing up: the Top 40. Joe's parents hated rock 'n' roll, but because they knew that Joe would be working for man that Joe looked up to and that they trusted, John Mounteer, they let Joe do the show. They made it perfectly clear to Joe that if his grades suffered as a result of these late nights, he would have to give up the radio show. Not a chance. Joe's grades improved, and his career began to take flight.

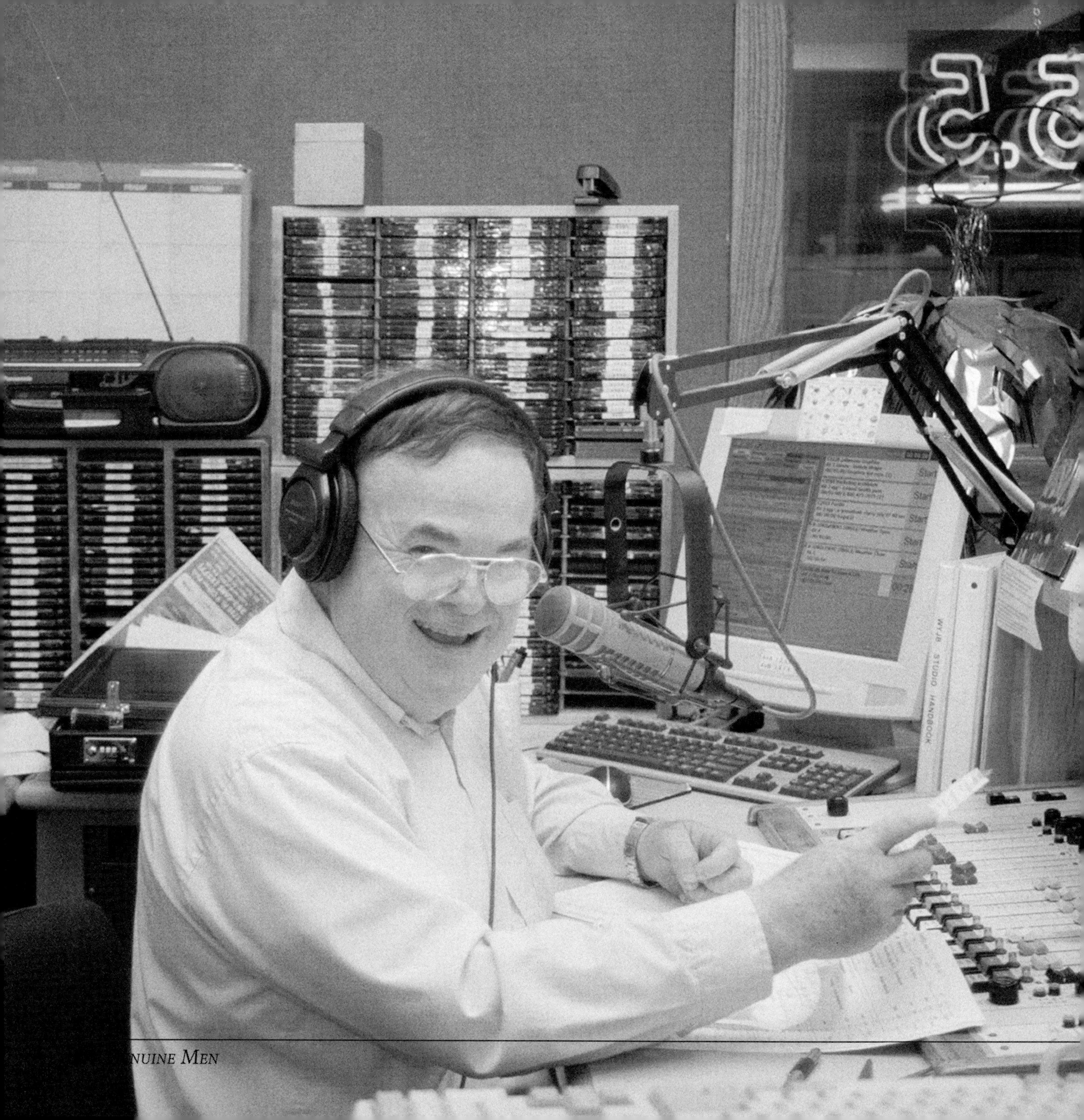
WYJB STUDIO HANDBOOK

Forty-five years later, his favorite time of day is still when he is on the radio, whether it is playing music or doing his public service program. Over the years media outlets have changed their formats and their focus, but Joe never forgot what drew him to the radio. He is painfully aware that the sound of his voice combined with honest words and a radio tower is a very powerful thing. It can hurt a person's feelings, it can change a person's point of view, it can win or lose an election for a candidate, and it can make a better day for a complete stranger. His listeners respond to him; they respect him; they count on him for much more than their favorite songs.

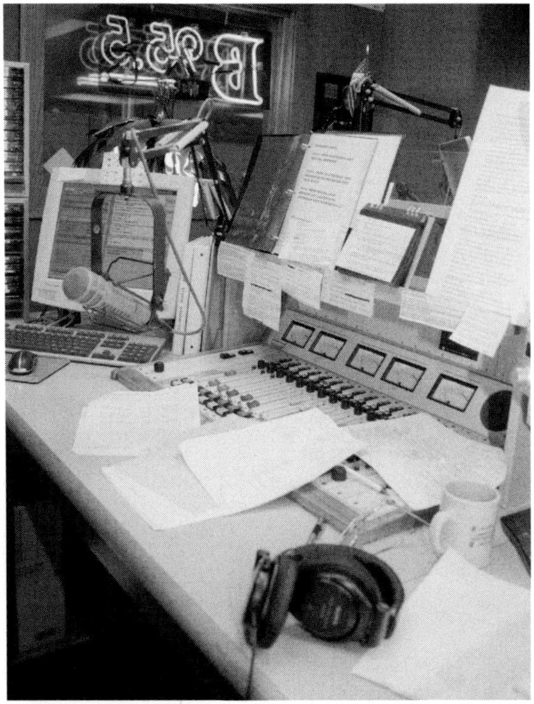

He is humble about it all—he sees himself as someone completely different. In his mind's eye, he is a little boy watching his grandfather pull out of the train station driving the Twentieth Century Limited, a magnificent train. He is the young man who married the girl of his dreams, and together they are the proud parents of a police officer. He is the broken grandson that had to learn how to go on living without his grandmother sitting and talking with him on the porch. He is a man surrounded by treasured friends, many of whom have been in his life since high school. He loves music; it is impossible to speak of Joe without recognizing that piece of him. He is forever grateful to the gift of music and broadcasting; they are the vehicles that have allowed him to learn about himself, challenge himself, and express himself. As Joe sees it, the greatest thing about music is that it has allowed him to bring humanity into the world.

The Gatekeeper

The day Ken was appointed Gatekeeper, there was no ceremony or celebration. In fact, it was considered by many observers simply to be a changing of the guard within an administration. His responsibility was to protect, rebuild, and maintain the bridges, tunnels, ports, and airports of the Port Authority. He was the watchman who stayed up nights so families could sleep safely in their homes. His was one of the honored voices speaking on behalf of a city, state, and nation at funerals honoring lives lost in the line of duty that fateful morning. He was the appointed team leader charged with moving forward while not getting caught up in bipartisan finger-pointing about the past. He was a facilitator for change, bringing the right people together to solve very challenging issues, many never faced in this lifetime. There was no single role that could have prepared him for these daunting responsibilities.

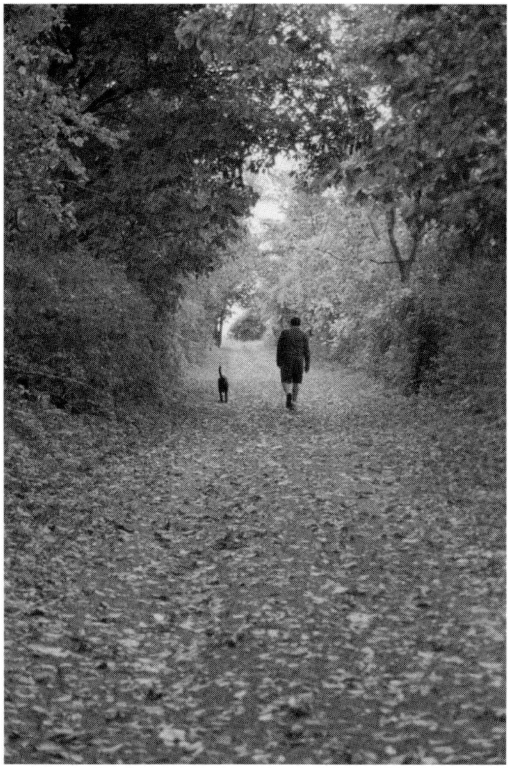

Ken began working in politics as a college student organizing a campus event for a mayoral candidate. He loved supporting those who embodied the spirit of public service. After college his first job was as a New York State government employee, but he chose to leave to run his family's business. Everything he learned in the bowling business helped him throughout his career in government and politics. As a business owner, it was natural for him to be

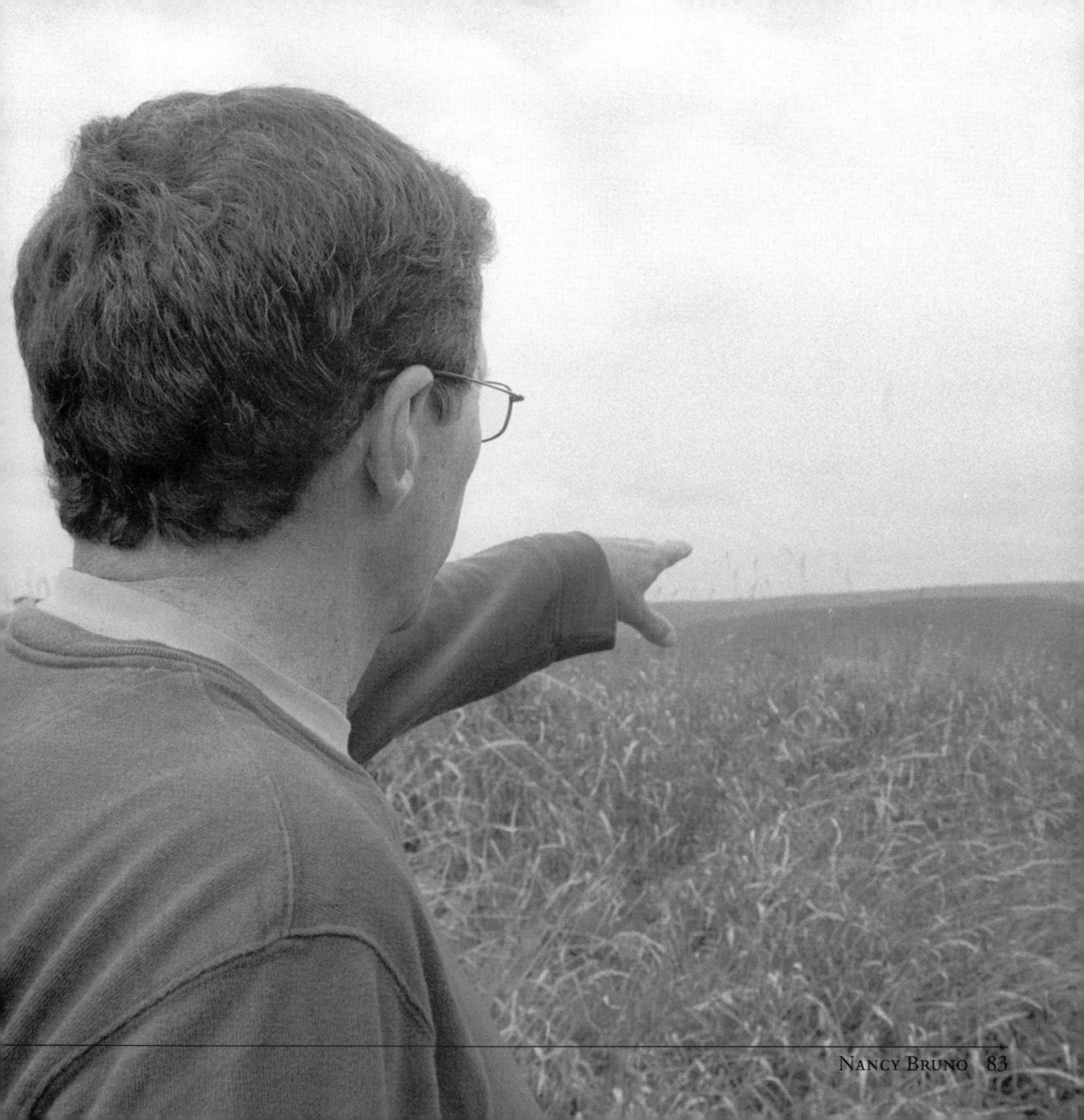

involved in his community. He began serving in local positions and rose to serve in very public roles. He was always earning the respect of his colleagues and his opponents for being tough but fair, building bipartisan relationships, and seeking the greatest good for those he served.

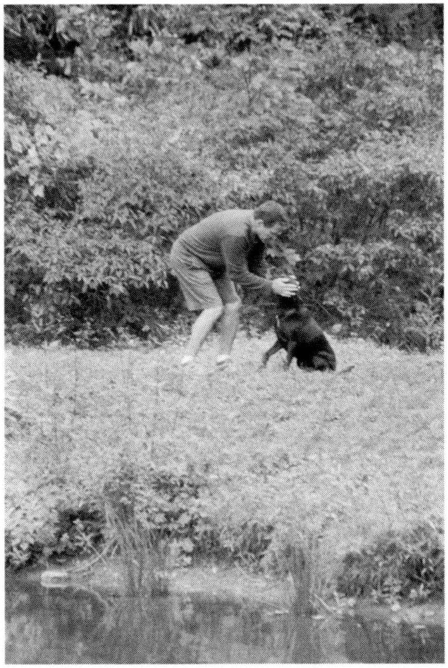

Then came the fateful day in September. The irony is that if he could change one thing in his life, it would be that 9/11 never occurred. Yet, if it didn't happen he would have never learned some of the most poignant lessons of his life, overcome some of the greatest challenges he faced professionally and personally, or come face-to-face with true heroes. He would not be the man he is today.

As he always planned, Ken handed the keys over to the new Gatekeeper; it was time to go home. That is the thing about The Gatekeeper: he is just a man. Ken is a husband and a father who is hoping soon to become a grandfather. He needs to exercise to stay in shape, he has two dogs, and he likes to play golf, ski, and hike. All of that takes a backseat when you are The Gatekeeper. Now it's Ken's turn to enjoy his family, sleep soundly in his home, let others make the tough decisions, and figure out what he will do next.

Running for Life

Pat was always quite athletic. He has participated in baseball, basketball, wrestling, and golf. Pat's mother was a swimmer, and his father ran track in college. Pat found that he was good at running and quite competitive amongst his peers. After high school, Pat competed at the collegiate level, running both cross country and track and winning his first state championship title in his sophomore year. Aware that he was a better long-distance runner, he became intrigued by endurance events. Following college, Pat began training for marathons, challenging his body to see what it was capable of doing, but always respectful of its limits.

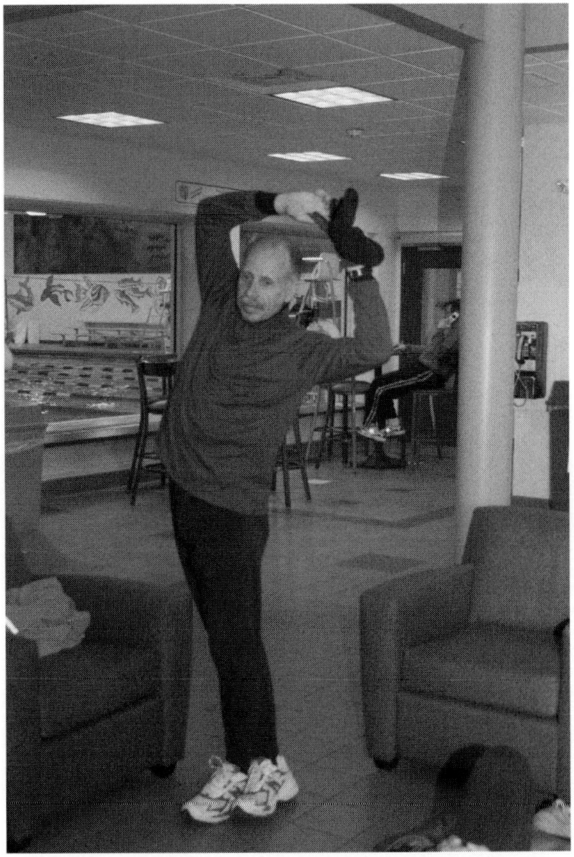

After he became an elementary school teacher, Pat primarily trained by himself after school. He hooked up with other runners on weekends for the longer distance runs that were a necessary part of marathon training. At twenty-nine he ran his first marathon in Philadelphia with the goal of qualifying for the Boston Marathon, his personal Holy Grail. In 1976, Pat ran the first of his nine Boston Marathons, and at the age of forty-two he chose to complete his marathon career where it all began. During this span of time, Pat ran a total of twenty-four marathons in the United States and Canada. These days Pat competes as a member of a competitive masters team and serves as a high school and USA Track and Field official.

Pat was lucky; he discovered something early in his life that he was successful at and found ways to incorporate it into his life. In exchange for his dedication to the sport, running has

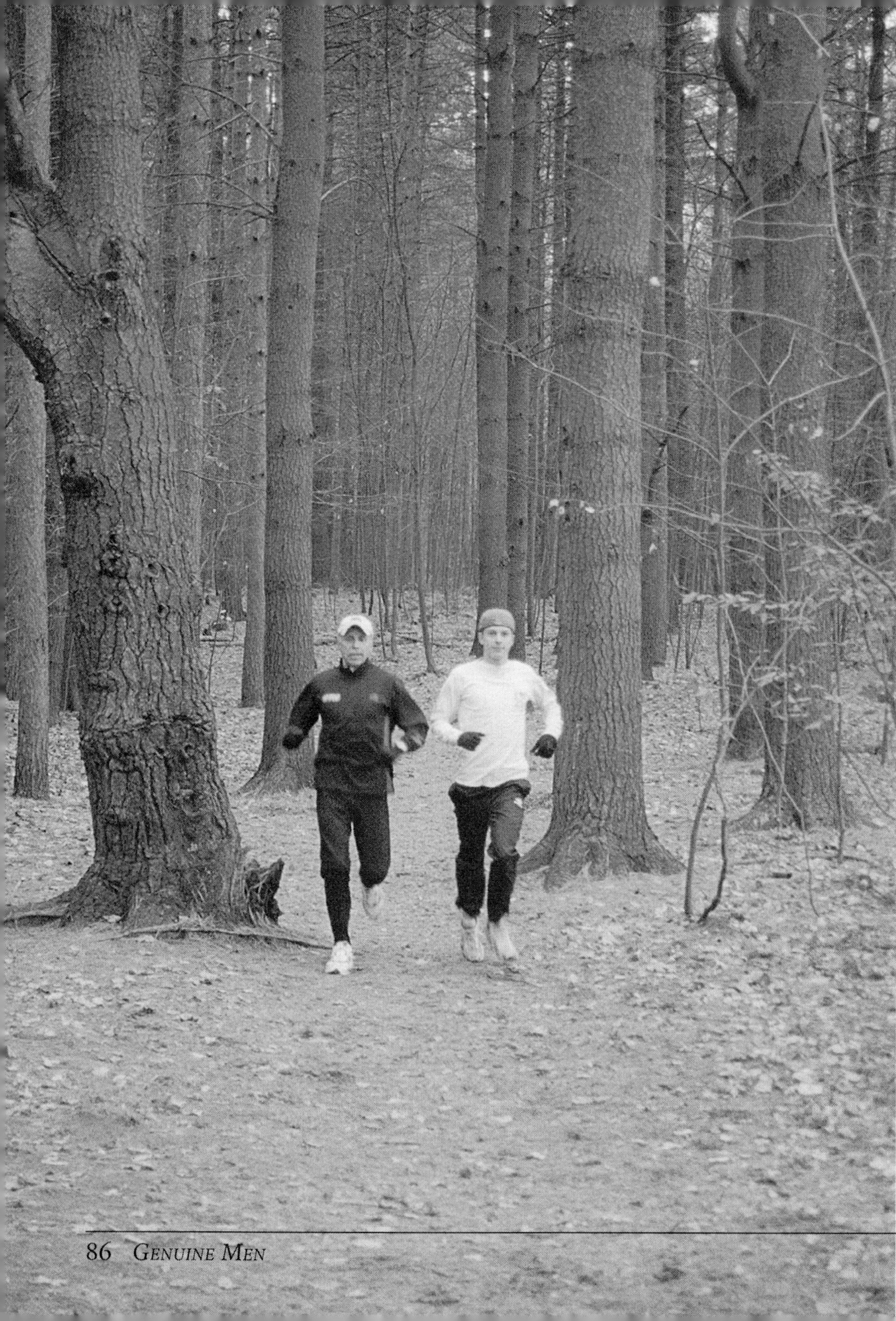

given Pat so many gifts. In high school and college, running gave him focus and self-esteem. When he was a young man it gave him the endurance that he needed during his army training and active service. During his teaching days it gave him an outlet after a long day in the classroom. And when he was a cancer patient it gave him a sense of normalcy when life didn't feel so normal. It also gave him something to share with his children: time together as they ran mile after mile, side by side. Some of the proudest moments of Pat's life are related to running: breaking two hours and thirty minutes in a marathon after several attempts, completing the Pike's Peak Ascent, watching his daughter complete her first NYC marathon, and witnessing his son win his first cross country invitational competition.

In one's lifetime there are so many things that you are encouraged to do, should do, and have to do. It is nice when just one of those things turns out to be something that you like. It is even better when you are actually good at it, and it is amazing when it is something that you are able to pursue your entire life.

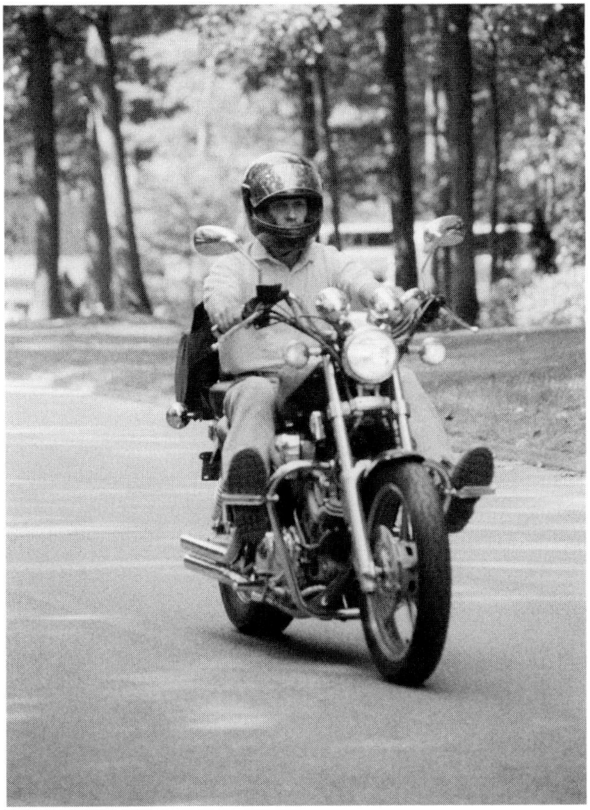

Life Is What You Make It

As a kid playing kick the can out in the street, he never dreamed he would one day be living in a penthouse and drinking his morning coffee while looking out on the ocean. His father worked twelve-hour days, seven days a week, as a cab driver to support his family. As a child, Al was aware that his family didn't have as much as the other families on the street, but his family had the most love. He remembers nights walking in the lightly falling snow up to the department store on the top of the hill. There was no extra money to be spent, but with his hand hooked into the arm of his mom's fake fur coat, feeling her reassuring strength, it really didn't matter. He was the happiest and most loved boy in the world.

At the age of seventeen the father of a classmate told him, "Buddy, you can be anything that you want to be." Because he idolized Mr. Anderson, for the first time in his life he believed every word. His father wanted him to take up a trade, but Al decided to join the Navy. As a "white hat," he found himself always replying, "Yes, sir," and "No, sir," to the men with big college rings. He realized that he was just as smart and ambitious, probably more so, than the men with the big college rings, and if he didn't want to spend the rest of his life saying, "Yes, sir," "No, sir," he needed to get a college education. Upon returning home from the service, he married, had three children, and juggled a full-time job and a full course load to earn his bachelor's degree. He became intrigued and excited about an industry that was truly on the brink of the unknown: computers. An entrepreneur at heart, he was not afraid of stepping off of the edge, or of failing. And he did both, but when things didn't go his way he simply would get up, lick his wounds, and ask, "What is next?"

It is true that money and power change people, but Al made sure never to forget where he came from: a loving home where people were treated firmly and with kindness. He is proof that business and human kindness can coexist. He was a benevolent dictator. There were times he had to take a hard line, say things that people may not have wanted to hear, and make difficult decisions. Regardless,

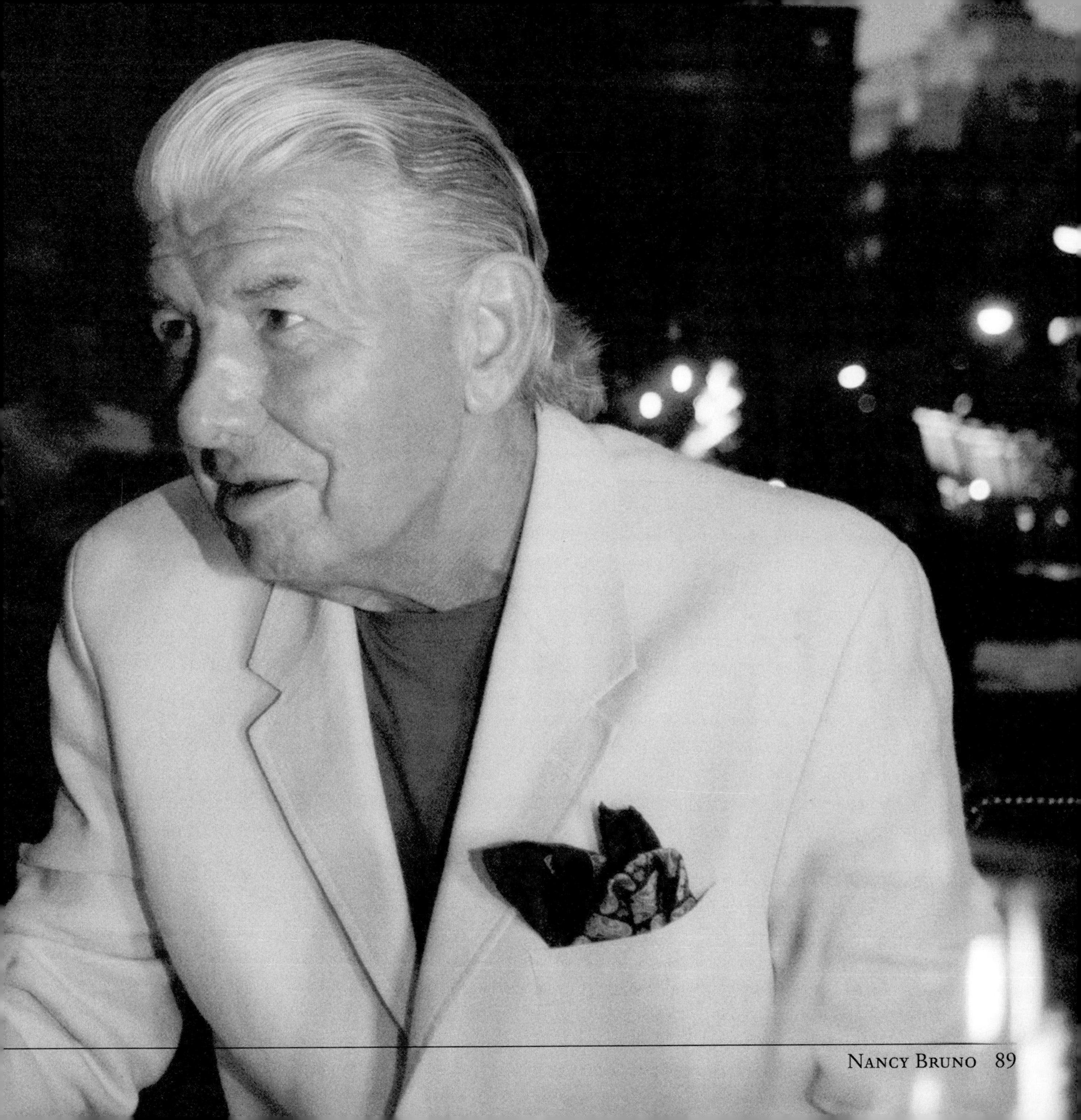

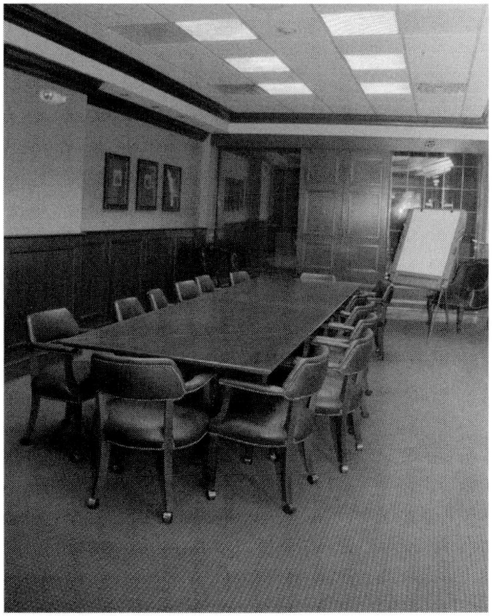

he approached every detail of his life with kindness and humanity. He did what he believed, at the time and with the information at his disposal, to be what was truly in everyone's best interest.

Al won't deny that one of his primary motivations to succeed was simply making money—a lot of it. He carried with him the memory of the little boy standing outside the department store, only able to look through the windows. His acquisitions were not made to impress others or to ingratiate himself with society; they were simply to satisfy the little boy who could only window-shop. Just in the last few years he has been cured of his need to buy; he no longer feels the *need* to acquire any more trinkets. He has come to realize that they mean nothing on the canvas of the Universe or the history of his life. He truly and finally understands and appreciates money for what it really represents: opportunities to achieve what others may see as impossible.

Now he indulges himself by reading the biographies of great leaders: Napoleon, Patton, Churchill, FDR, Teddy Roosevelt, Henry Ford, and Ronald Reagan. He enjoys his daily exercise routine, beef carpaccio, and reading the *National Review* and *Weekly Standard* cover to cover. Don't be mistaken—his appetite is still insatiable. He wishes he could be the King of Jordan. This wish has absolutely nothing to do with having the trappings of a king, but with wanting to help make a positive impact on the world stage. For now, he is content with looking out at the ocean from his kitchen window. Glancing down at his simple pad of paper he looks over the items on his "must do" list that are incomplete. Looking onto the horizon, he asks himself, "What is next?" And with that in mind, he picks up his pen and begins to add on to his list. The way he sees it, it is just a good race with time to get them all checked off.

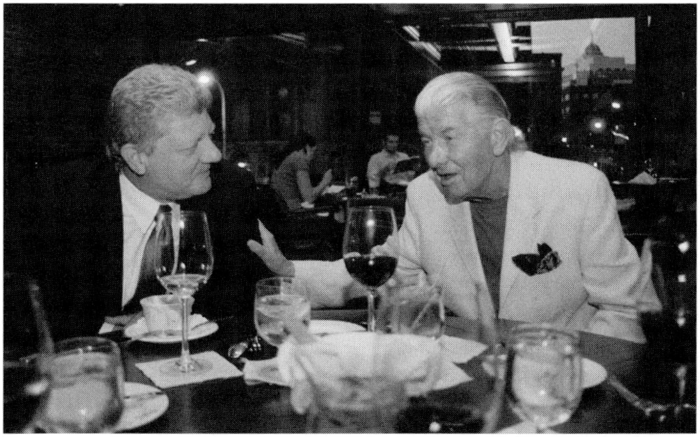

IT'S THE LITTLE THINGS ALONG THE WAY

As Bill reflects back upon his life, he would be remiss if he didn't believe that he is a truly fortunate man. Through every stage of his life he has been surrounded by people who have made a significant impact on him: strong and caring parents; siblings who are also friends and confidantes; teachers and priests; his wonderful and supportive wife, Jane; and his three daughters, each smart, talented, and successful in their own right.

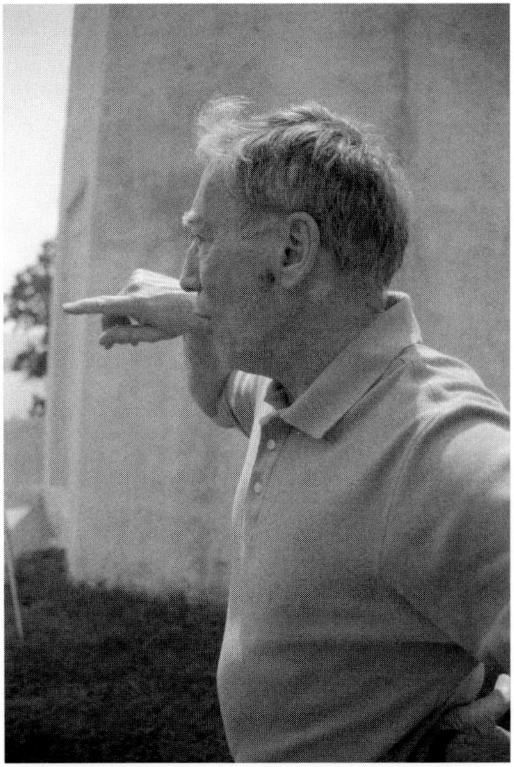

He was a good student, and he attended Cardinal Hayes High School, graduated, and went to college. After graduation, he decided to push up his draft, fulfilling his military obligation before looking for a job. After basic training, he was sent on to special training where he acquired many new skills, including learning to type. Bill was sent to Frankfurt, Germany, where part of his duties as an Army clerk involved giving Troop Information and education classes to other soldiers. It never crossed his mind that this part of his army experience could play an important role in his life's work. After being discharged from the Army, he heard a radio commercial for a new Master's in Education program especially designed for college graduates who had not had any other education credits. Intrigued, he took note of it and tucked it away in the back of his mind. It was the summer of 1960, and he had a job working for the Internal Revenue Service, which was a decent job and a way to pay the bills. Remembering the commercial he

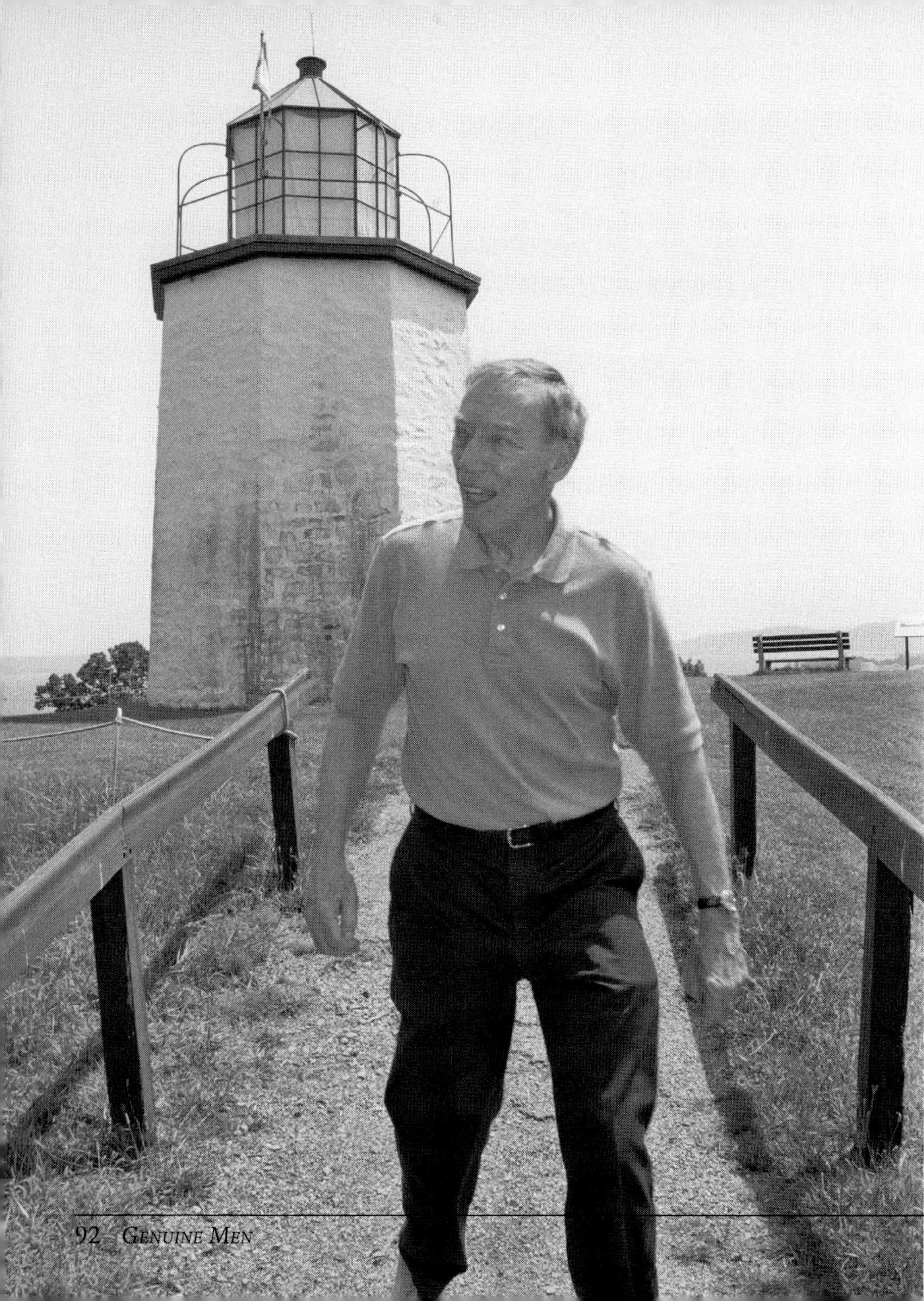

had heard for the teaching program, he enrolled at Fordham University in the summer of 1962.

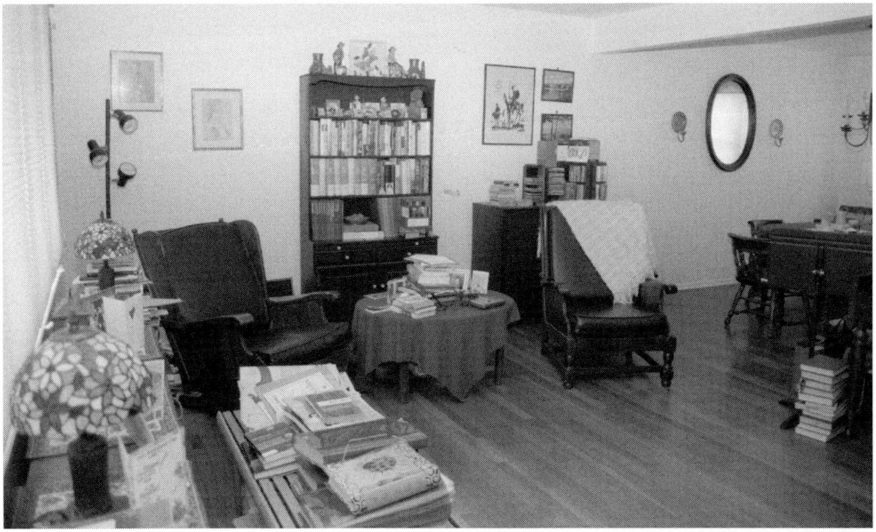

He accepted his first teaching position the following September. The school needed a long-term substitute who could teach an odd combination of history and typing. As it happened, history had always been his best subject in school, and thanks to his army career he was able to accept the job. Teaching quickly developed from a job to a career, and after two years as a teacher in New York City, he and Jane moved out of the city, and Bill began teaching at a high school where he remained for thirty years. As an educator, Bill viewed his role as giving him an opportunity to challenge young people to think logically and develop informed opinions. With this in mind, it was important to create a classroom atmosphere where students were open to different ideas and treated one another as equals. The way people treat one another is the one thing that he wishes he could improve upon, and he tried to do his part for five periods a day. Upon retiring from his high school position, Bill missed the excitement of the classroom and taught for five years as an adjunct professor of history at a community college.

Forever faced with the challenge of making the proper use of his abilities, Bill considers himself lucky to have found in education a profession that fit so well with his personal strengths. On the walls of his office are family photos, books, and letters from students. He changed their lives, he made them think differently about history and themselves, and he made a positive impact. Teaching is a part of his life, his family, and part of how he defines himself as a man.

Stories from the Past

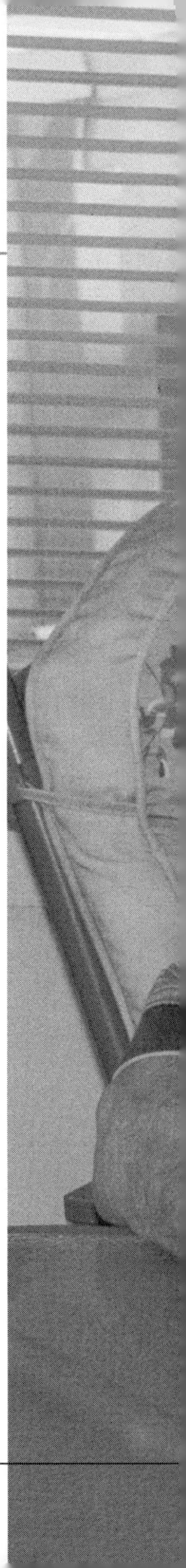

John begins each morning with a prayer. The Lord has been good to him: strong and loving parents, a devoted wife, and wonderful children and grandchildren. Throughout his lifetime they have given him so many gifts, and he has repaid them with the legacy of his stories. He learned the power of storytelling from his father, a man filled with common-sense anecdotes that he applied to life's problems. Knowing what this did for him, John shares his stories, believing that each one helps his loved ones on their life's journey.

John often reflects back upon his childhood. There are so many memories and lessons he learned from his parents. They modeled what it meant to be parents and spouses through good times and bad, sickness and health, how to be accepting and appreciative of others' generosity, and how to keep your head held high through the most difficult of times. Weekends were always a special time for John and his father: taking trips into New York City, watching boxers work out at Stillman's Gym, and walking through Central Park, where his dad would point out projects that he worked on as an iron worker.

Many lessons came out of the Great Depression, and as John grew to be a man, his parents instilled in him that no matter what he did in life to always do a good job, take a steady job, be the head of the family, and respect the value of a dollar. It has been over seventy years since those days, but John can look back and say that he has lived his life and raised his family with the values passed on to him from his parents.

In the Army, during World War II, he was responsible for fixing radios for Piper Cub aircraft. The lives of pilots and artillery field men depended on him to do a good job. He returned home and went to the Veterans Vocational School on the GI Bill and studied radio communication. He could fix anything and was able to get a well-paying job. John met a beautiful young woman named Geraldine through his younger sister, and the proudest day of his life was the day they married in September of 1954. Not long after, with money he saved from the Army, they purchased a house

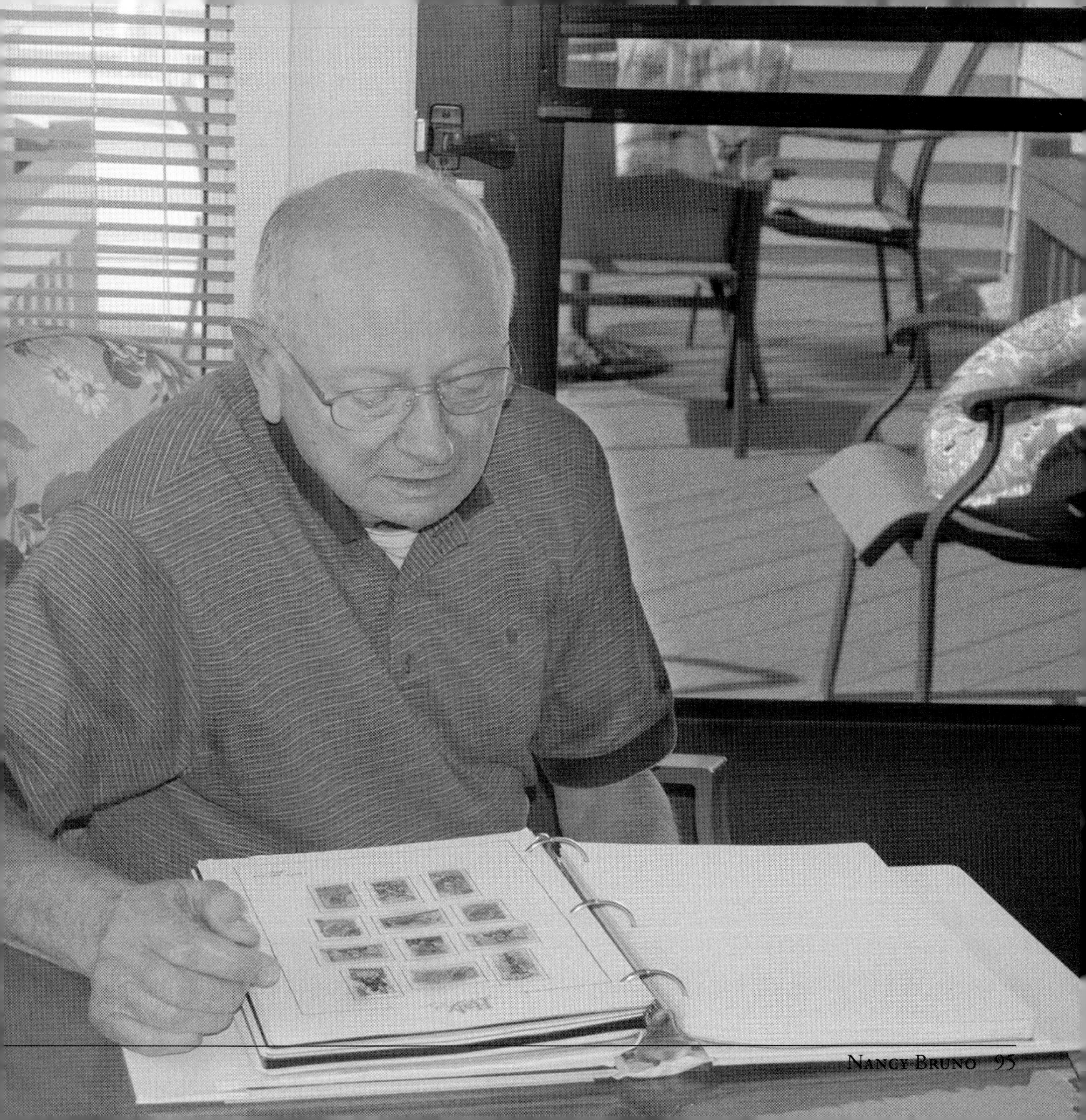

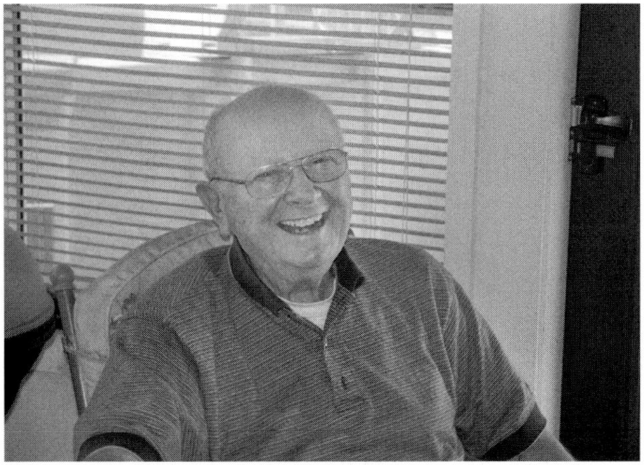

that would become the home in which they raised their five children. It is the only home they have ever known. Remembering how much Saturdays with his father meant to him, he continued the Saturday tradition with his children, bringing one or two with him on Saturday service calls. It wasn't hard to find an assistant; they all knew that at the end of the day John would stop at the local bakery for bread and treats.

After twenty-three years in a stable job, but having no pension, John decided to enter a new field at the age of forty-four. In the short term he had no choice but to take home less money, but the long-term rewards meant a better future for his family. On his last day of work, he walked out of the building and shouted, "Free At Last!" And those words bring him to the story of his grandfather, an Italian immigrant who moved to Land of the Free: America. John believes in inherited memories, abilities, and knowledge passed down through the generations. Maybe they are family characteristics, maybe they are things that were taught to him that he just doesn't remember learning, or maybe they are lessons and morals from stories told to him by someone who thought they would serve him well on his life's journey. Regardless of what it is called, it began for him with his grandfather, who passed it on to his father, and it now runs through John, who is making sure that it continues through his children and grandchildren.

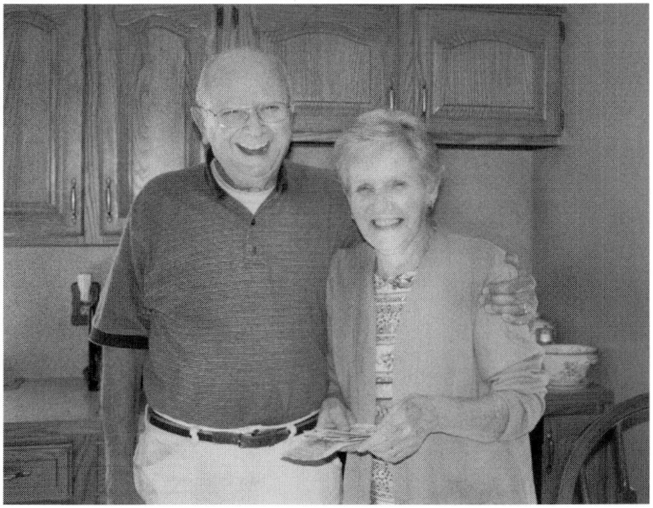

A Living Legacy

Sanford's mother devoted herself to everyone—her family, friends, neighbors, strangers, absolutely anyone who needed her help. She gave without a thought or an expectation of receiving anything in return. Sanford's father was a quiet man, but when he spoke people listened to him intently. He was a cattle dealer who built and maintained a reputation as an honorable man around the country and, most importantly, in his own community. Sanford recognized very early in life that he was a fortunate young man: the Great Depression was a time of moderation, not survival; his family was one of the first to have a television in their home; his parents paid for his college tuition and sent him twenty-five dollars every week. He often wondered why he deserved all of this, and he never took any of it for granted. Instead, he knew that the most fitting way to repay his parents was to emulate them by helping others.

He was drafted in 1943 at the age of eighteen and left his sophomore year of college to enter the Army. Knowing his son's nature, his father's parting words were, "Do your job, but don't be a hero." It never entered Sanford's mind that he would be killed. He was assigned to the Fifth Air Force Division and shipped off to the Southwest Pacific. Always wise beyond his years, Sanford assumed the role of counselor to frightened young soldiers. Throughout his years in the service, Sanford was the one who they would seek out to discuss their problems, ask their questions, express their fears, or just to talk. Sanford knew what he was doing provided his friends and comrades comfort and peace of mind. Afterward, Sanford returned to the United States, graduated from college, and chose to enter law school. Sanford was not interested in being a lawyer, but with nothing else sparking his interest and the government footing the bill, he began to attend classes.

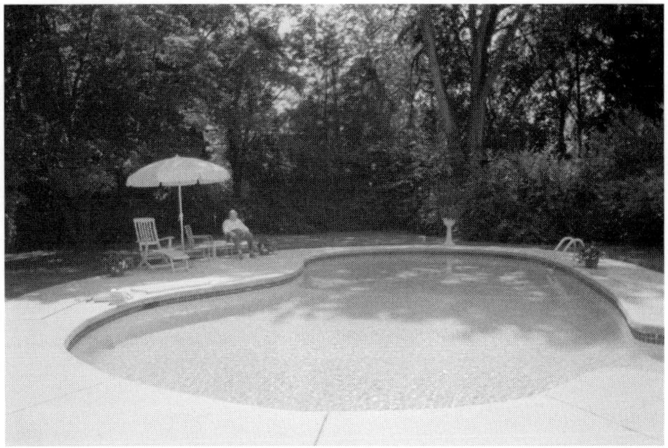

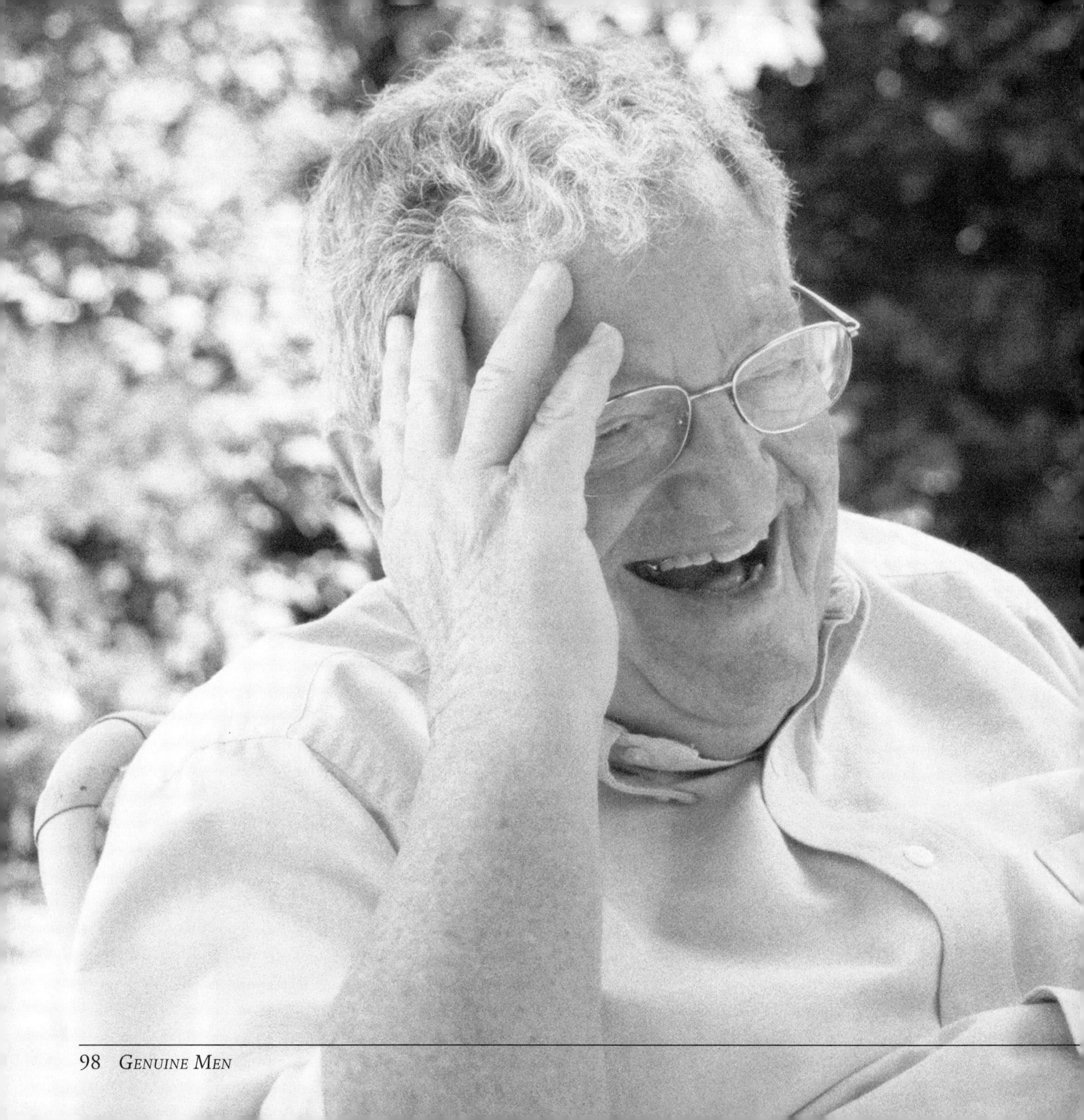

Four years went by, and over time, guys he thought would make good lawyers were forced to leave law school, unable to pass their final exams. Yet Sanford, a man still unsure what he was going to do with a law degree, kept passing the exams and returning to continue his studies at the beginning of each new semester. A month before graduation, Sanford stood before a mock court and argued his first case. Discovering his passion within that courtroom was transformational. Armed this time with a law degree instead of a gun, Sanford was ready once again to discuss problems, find answers to questions, and protect people in their time of fear and uncertainty.

When Sanford began practicing law, many attorneys preferred not take on matrimonial cases. Because of its complicated and complex nature, matrimonial law took up a great deal of a lawyer's time; it just wasn't as lucrative as other areas of the law. His joy was helping to create families through adoption, but his strength was the compassionate dissolution of the marriage contract. Sanford always operated from the mindset that any divorce was a tragedy, and he was there to help his clients get through this difficult and complicated process. As a matrimonial lawyer, he took on many roles: an attorney protecting his clients under the law and ensuring a fair settlement; a marriage counselor working through private and painful issues; and a social worker looking out for the best interest of children. Many of his clients were women unable to afford representation. When no one else would take them on as clients, they turned up on Sanford's doorstep. They were always warmly and respectfully greeted by Sanford asking, "How can I help?"

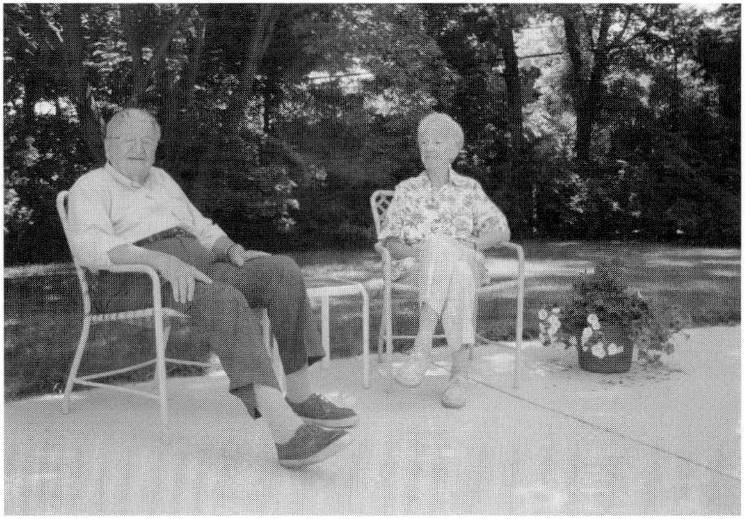

For a man never interested in being a lawyer, for fifty-seven years Sanford was a magnificent counselor of the law. He has honored his parent's legacy by taking what he was passionate for in his life and using it to serve others, expecting little or nothing in return.

Once a Marine, Always a Marine

Jim was just twenty years old when the Japanese bombed Pearl Harbor in December of 1941. He was desperate to join the United States Marine Corps, and he needed his mother to sign the papers allowing him to enlist. When he entered the Corps, the Marine values of Honor, Courage, and Commitment became the bedrock of his character and the foundation by which he chose to lead his life. Jim reported for duty January 7, 1942, at 90 Church Street in New York City and then headed south by train to Parris Island for boot camp. Due to the need of combat troops, his boot camp training was shortened, and Jim was assigned to Fleet Marine Force, Company M, Third Battalion, First Marine Division. On August 7, 1942, Jim and his battalion made the initial landing on Guadalcanal. Jim was a machine gunner, carrying fifty pounds of steel on his back, and embraced his responsibilities with vigor and enthusiasm.

Marines define courage by "what you are in the dark," and these young men demonstrated what they were made of in the jungles of the Solomon Islands. Under constant enemy fire and bombings from the airplanes in the skies above, it was all these young men could do to survive. With the constant bombardment, it could be up to thirteen days before any reinforcements could come to their assistance. It was during these times in the dark that Jim learned to develop moral strength and mental discipline, began listening to his inner voice, and began holding himself accountable to a higher standard. The Marines never gave up, never gave in, and never willingly accepted second best against their enemy, and five months later they secured that island from the Japanese.

Throughout his lifetime, Jim has built an uncompromising code of personal integrity based on the concept of being a United States Marine. A critical part of Marine training is embracing the concept of *semper fidelis*, translated from Latin meaning "Always Faithful." As a husband and father

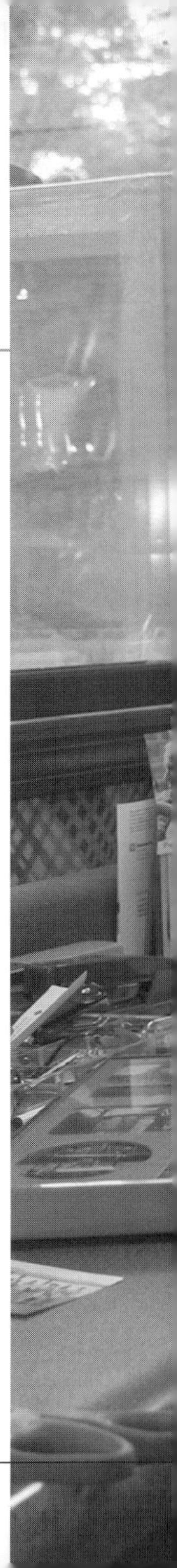

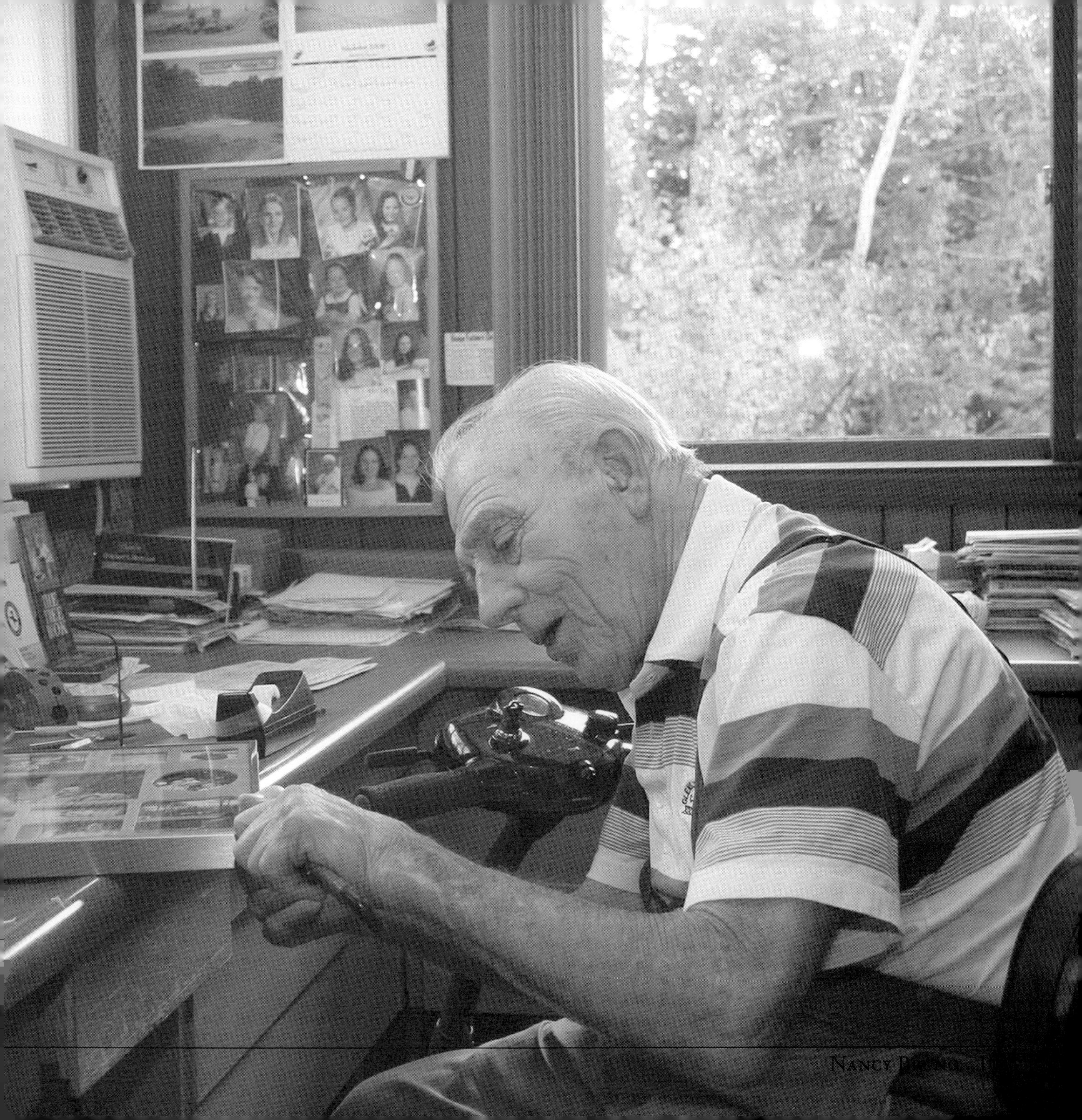

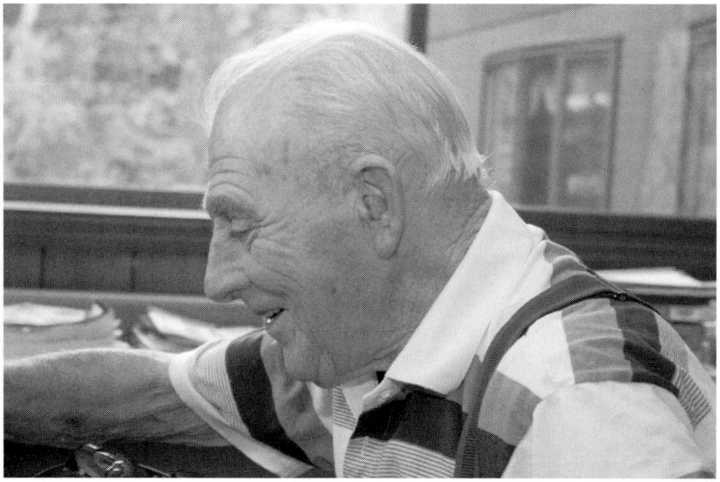

of two daughters, Jim always operated from a place of truth. He has honored his wife, and like the Marine's English bulldog mascot, has remained fiercely loyal to her throughout their sixty-two years of marriage.

The Chinese used the term "gung ho," meaning working together, to describe Marines in China around 1900. The term conveys a willingness to tackle any task, and that is exactly what Jim did when he moved to Upstate New York to begin a new life. It was Jim's vision to take a wooded tract of land and turn it into a family resort. Although he had the vision, everyone pulled together to make his dream a reality. All for one, one for all. The family business has just completed its thirty-eighth year. He has never walked away from this or any other commitment he has made in his lifetime.

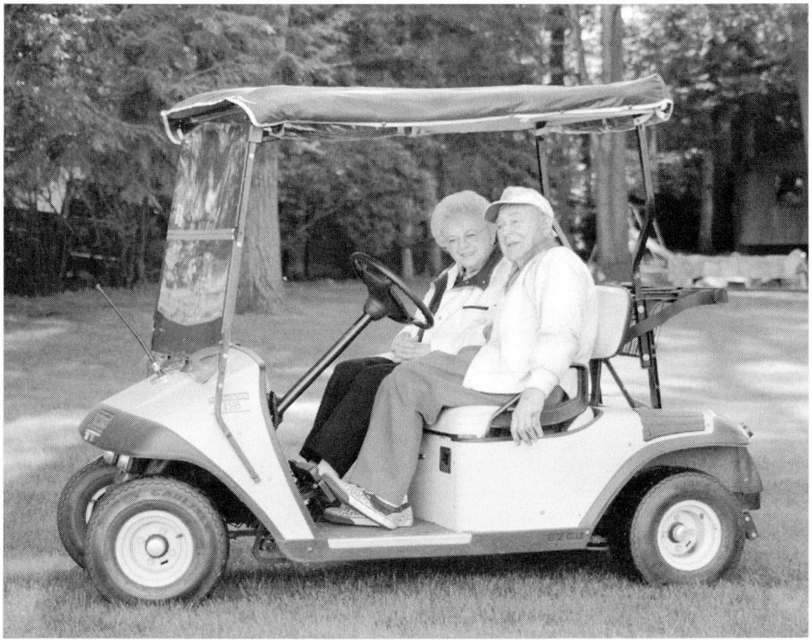

Jim has held the title of Marine for sixty-five years; there are no ex-Marines or former Marines. Each day as he looks in the mirror, he is proud to see a man that served his country and family with selfless determination and total dedication. Once a Marine, always a Marine. Commitment never dies.

Along the Way

Gino is a ninety-one-year-old rock star. He signs autographs and poses for pictures with business leaders at golf tournaments and college students at basketball games. His admirers range in age from eighteen to eighty. What is he famous for? Being Gino.

At the age of eight Gino's older brother brought him to the private country club he worked at as a caddy and taught him the game of golf. Gino played all different kinds of sports growing up, but to him there was nothing like golf. School wasn't Gino's thing; his eyesight was very bad, and it was hard for him to read and study. Instead, he got his education from the lawyers, doctors, and businessmen he listened to as he carried their bags along an eighteen-hole round of golf. He never forgot a thing he heard on the course. At seventeen Gino was recruited to drive an ambulance up and down the eastern seaboard for the Civilian Conservation Corp. The hours on the road were long and lonely. There were many New York State Troopers' barracks along his route where Gino always found a hot meal, warm bed, and good conversation. He never forgot the kindness the Troopers showed him as a young man.

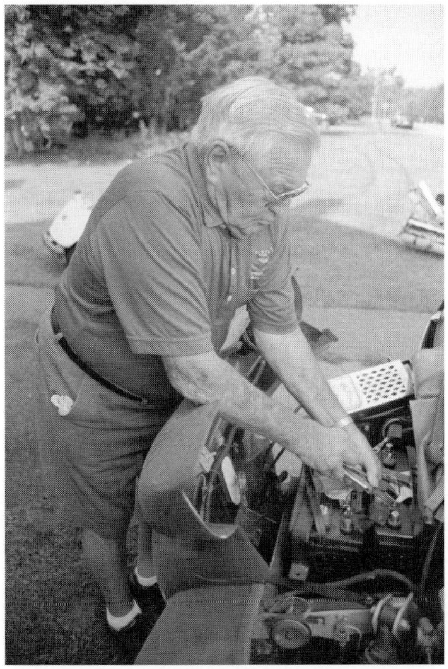

Gino met his wife, Willie, at a roller skating party. She was a farmer's daughter who was strong and beautiful, had good values, and made great pie. They married and had a boy they called Gigi. Gigi was a great kid, but he was a boy growing up in a city, and Gino was working long hours to make ends meet. The local YMCA was a haven where Gigi learned gymnastics, was a stand out on the swim team, went to summer camp, and learned to respect himself and others in his community. Gino would never forget the role the YMCA played in his son's upbringing. While working for the Exxon Oil Company, a vice president encouraged him to go to college so he could join the Exxon sales force. Gino had to decline the offer because he was

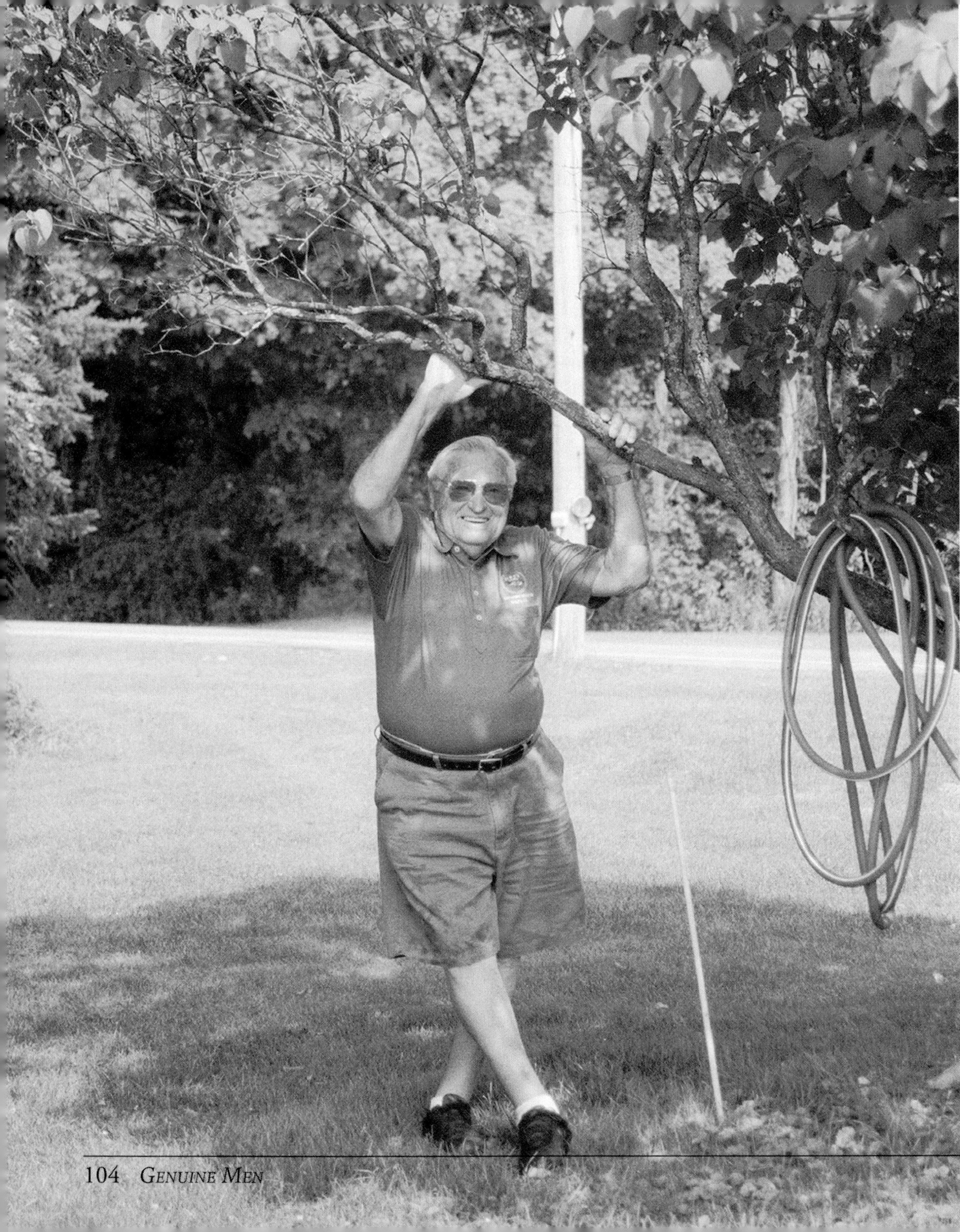

never able to finish high school, but he never forgot that someone saw that he had the drive to succeed. That drive is what helped take a dream, make it a vision, and transform it into a reality. Some say Gino achieved the impossible: he took a tract of farmland and a borrowed bulldozer and single-handedly created a nine-hole golf course in the middle of the winter. He told his creditors that the only way he was going to be able to make his course a success was if he didn't pay them for two years. He never forgot that they never asked him for a dime during that period. He paid off his loans on time, expanded the course to eighteen holes, and ran it as a semi-private golf club with his wife and son for over twenty years.

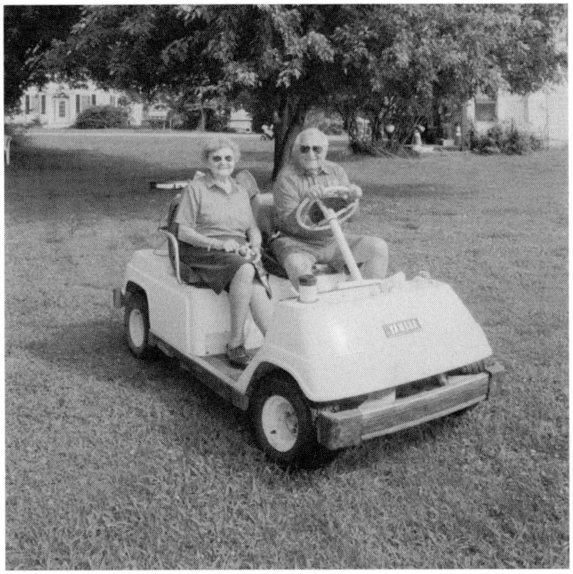

Life took a tragic turn when he and Willie lost Gigi, who by that time was a successful lawyer and businessman. Gino was determined to make sure that no one would forget Gigi. Gino and Willie felt that a golf scholarship for boys and girls was a fitting tribute. Over the years, Gino and Willie have become surrogate parents and grandparents to the college athletes, coaches, faculty, and staff of Siena College. Their enthusiasm is infectious; there is a buzz when they are around campus. The students enjoy them as much as they enjoy being with the students. They attend games, provide moral support, Willie has become the unofficial statistician for the basketball teams, and Gino fixes the electric cars that patrol campus. They have given the school a great deal more than their money; they have given their family's spirit.

Gino and Willie had no expectations when they created the scholarship, but in return for their gift they have received an entirely new life. Gino has learned to read, earned his high school diploma at the age of eighty, and earned an honorary doctorate in Humane Letters. His social schedule is packed with dinners with friends and admirers, fundraisers for the college, attending athletic events, and of course playing a lot of golf. He has never forgotten where he came from and how, in his times of need, there were people there to assist him and his family. He continues to make a difference, whether it is lending his name to raise funds for a worthy cause, changing a tire, selling a lawn mower for a friend, or giving a golf lesson. He has experienced the transformational power of generosity and compassion for others. Look at him: he's a rock star.